D1516131

To

Deanna
_____

From

Julie
_____

Date

Christmas 2022
_____

DEDICATION

I dedicate this book to my husband, J. Deon Reed.
Thank you for all the encouragement and support while writing
this book. Most of all, thank you for being my rock! I love you.

To my children, Olivia and Josiah. You're my greatest inspiration.
I thoroughly enjoy being your mom. I'm so grateful God told me
to come home to focus more on both of you!

BRIDGETTE REED

Release

90 DAYS TO EMBRACE
GOD'S PLAN FOR YOUR LIFE

DaySpring

LIVE YOUR FAITH

Published by:

21154 Highway 16 East
Siloam Springs, AR 72761
dayspring.com

CONTENTS

Hey, Faith Walker!

Do you feel unsettled as if your life wasn't lining up with God's plan for you? If so, I wrote this devotional for you. Through my own tears, hard times, and struggles, I was taught the lessons of walking by faith. You see, my professional aspirations and my motivations to move up in life never felt comfortable even though I knew I'd been training for a greater position my entire life. I was sure my life would be spent as a medical doctor or in a high-rise office in a senior position of a fortune 500 company. So how did I end up abandoning all my professional aspirations for one that God had for me? I walked away because God was letting me know that He had other plans. Was it easy? No. Did I question my worth? Absolutely. But today, I have experienced God in amazing, real ways that could have only happened through my following of His will for my life. It is my prayer that you would commit ninety days to seek God like never before. Read the devotions and prayers, but also go deeper into the Scriptures and make it your goal to have your time in prayer be longer and longer each day. I promise you won't regret it. Find a space for you and Jesus to commune each day. Set it up perfectly and meet with Him there. Even if it's in your car or on the train somewhere, make it your mission to seek God daily. Feel like you need to make a big change but don't know if you can do it? Let this book be your coach to walk you through each season of change. I divided the devotions into four seasons. These were the seasons I personally experienced when I stepped out into the unknown. I remember feeling (1) uncertain, feeling (2) vulnerable, and then needing (3) rest as I experienced (4) transformation. It didn't happen overnight, and your journey may take less or longer time than mine did. Just keep going. If you get stuck or distracted, come back to this book. Every Scripture has been handpicked for you in this season. Congrats! This book is your first step to becoming unstuck, and finding freedom!

– Bridgette Reed

Check Your Settings

Then He said to the crowd, "If any of you wants to be My follower, you must give up your own way, take up your cross daily, and follow Me. If you try to hang on to your life, you will lose it. But if you give up your life for My sake, you will save it. And what do you benefit if you gain the whole world but are yourself lost or destroyed?"

LUKE 9:23–25

Have you ever felt like the path you were on was off? That somehow you had taken a wrong turn? After college, I got a job as a traveling professional development trainer. On one occasion, I rented a vehicle and had to rent the GPS separately. Once I got into the car, I put the GPS on the dashboard mount. I put in the address of my location, and it stated that I had a six-and-a-half-hour drive. What happened next caught me off guard. I was driving in the direction the GPS told me to go, yet I found myself on dirt roads far away from highways. I drove by large farmlands in the middle of Ohio. I kept on the path the GPS told me to take until I realized that every major road I had come across was not part of my route. Instead, my GPS was taking me down back roads. I was headed to Cleveland, and my GPS was directing me down the longest road to get there. After inspecting the GPS, I realized it was set to "back roads only." Somehow, while the GPS was in my purse, I pressed buttons that set it on a path I was never intended to be on. Once I corrected the settings, I got to my destination by getting on the right road—which was quicker and smoother.

How often do we get into a car (which represents our lives) with a GPS (which represents the preselected settings of our mind and societal pressures) only to be driving in what feels like circles, unable to truly connect with the journey? In moments like these, God, in His love for us, will whisper, "Check the settings," as He did for me in real time. The programming of the world will often leave us feeling lost and confused, wondering, "Where am I?" Check the settings, my friend. When Jesus says you must give up your own way, He is saying, "Once you give up your life, your journey, and your way, and decide to do life My way, that is when you will find your way." I can't tell you it will be an easy or quick journey, but it will be the right one. This type of journey happened to me when I left my job to become a full-time mom and wife. Before I left, I reset my settings by deciding my life was no longer my own, and I gave up trying to live my way. Now it was time to do things God's way.

Prayer

God, redirect my thoughts to You every single day.
Redirect my motives. Redirect my desires.
Release me to follow Your plans and Your purpose for my life.
In Jesus' name. Amen.

God Goals

Do not love this world nor the things it offers you,
for when you love the world, you do not have the love of the
Father in you. For the world offers only a craving for physical
pleasure a craving for everything we see, and pride in our
achievements and possessions. These are not from the Father,
but are from this world. And this world is fading away,
along with everything that people crave. But anyone who
does what pleases God will live forever.

I JOHN 2:15–17

It happens every day. My four-year-old daughter wakes up, gets dressed, and rushes to the stairs. To her, walking down the stairs is a race that she MUST win at all costs. If I happen to walk down the stairs and get to the bottom faster than her, not trying to compete with her, I am met with a meltdown of proportions that will make any parent cringe. When I pick her up and ask, "What is wrong that requires this breakdown?" she looks at me and says, "I want to win! I want to be a winner." I look back at her and remind her that we are family—when one of us wins, we all win. I also share with her that walking down the stairs is not about winning but about getting to the destination safely. If we all run down the stairs, we could all get hurt.

In these moments with my daughter, I can't help thinking about the many times in my own life when the goal has been winning, achieving, striving, and trying to make things happen—only to be left overwhelmed, frustrated, and lost. This sensational craving for better, more, and higher becomes toxic to our growth. I recognized this not long after I had my children. As I gave up the striving, the winning, and the performance-driven lifestyle, I realized that it was no longer about me but about submission to a greater goal—a God goal. It was no longer about me winning but about fulfilling the mission God has for my life. That is when everything changed. My five-year plan evaporated as I fell into faith. I allowed God to take over in a way that at first felt like I was falling, but I was really learning how to truly trust in God. Faith and trust make up a daily journey that is now what I consider to be winning and succeeding—all in the safety of His plan over my own.

Prayer

Father, release my desire to live a performance-based lifestyle and keep my eyes focused on doing the next thing You told me to do with humility and patience. In Jesus' name. Amen.

Do the Dishes

Be on your guard; stand firm in the faith;
be courageous; be strong.

I CORINTHIANS 16:13 NIV

When God called me to be a stay-at-home wife and mom, I really didn't know what to expect. I had a semi-idea of what it would look like, but for the most part, this was the biggest leap of faith I had ever taken. As someone who had worked in some capacity since age twelve and who came from a working-parent household, this was a very unfamiliar area for me. I started getting the feeling to "come home" full-time after my daughter was born. Being a first-time mom of a newborn made me see life in such a different way. It was no longer just about me and my husband. I had a human depending wholly on me. Her tiny self and the health issues I experienced early in her life made me long to be with her at all times. I cried when I dropped her off for her first day of daycare and knew that my season of working full-time was coming to an end.

It took two-and-a-half years and one more child before I would transition home. Over the course of those years, God increased my desire to be home to a point where that is all I wanted to do. I just wanted to be a homemaker and create a peaceful, loving environment for my family. After speaking with my husband, and watching God shift my life so this could happen, I had a memorable first day at home. I heard God say, "Do the dishes." He said that to me because I woke up saying, "Okay God, it's Your plan now. How am I going to reach the nations for Your glory?" For some reason, it hadn't dawned on me yet that the purpose of that season was to be at home. A little confused, I thought, Is this what being a homemaker is all about? God, I need a plan to be a mompreneur! He said, "Go do the dishes." Perplexed and a bit confused, I went to do the dishes. As I was doing the dishes, I heard my phone buzz. It was an opportunity I never even sought out. I thought to myself, I simply did the dishes and God provided. That is when I first learned to be on guard, stand firm in the faith, and be courageous.

Being on guard meant not being distracted by worldly things or what society says I should be doing, but instead keeping my mind focused to think of Him and what He tells me to do. I woke up every day to pray, to read my devotional and Bible, and to meditate on His Scripture. That was a part of the reprogramming of my mind. Standing firm in the faith became an action word based upon my response to His direction. Being courageous was simply about knowing. Knowing that He is God and that I can trust Him in all circumstances.

Prayer

Father, I don't know what the future holds, but You do. Release my need to do things my way and my need to know the plans. Lead and guide me every step, and give me courageous faith. In Jesus' name. Amen.

God has a Plan

The Lord Himself will fight for you. Just stay calm.

EXODUS 14:14

Just stay calm. How often do we allow our circumstances to throw us into a frenzy of overwhelm, panic, and anxiety? The whirlwind and turmoil of an unexpected situation, a great disappointment, and the unknown have led many of us to feel like we have lost control. But did we ever have control? The thing about embracing uncertainty is that it is at the core of embracing our trust in our Lord. He promises us that He will fight for us. As the good Father that He is, His love will always go before us to protect us, guide us, and fight for us. We must be prepared for the unexpected. That preparation isn't necessarily a full-blown plan—A, B, C, or D—but a position of your heart, your will to rest, and your decision to trust God no matter what happens.

We always hope for the best and for things to go our way, but when they don't, we must know that God has a plan. He is always in control when life unfolds around us. When things don't go our way, maybe our response should be: "God, I guess You have another plan because this is not going how I imagined. I can't wait to see what You're up to." He knows what is happening in the spiritual realm, and He knows what we can handle. For the person who is in the middle of panicking, unable to stop the tears and worry from flowing, hold on to this promise and today's Scripture. It might feel like it's all you have to hold on to, but God will never fail you. The only thing that can never fail us is the Word of God. Speak it back to Him: "God, You said You will fight for me. Help me to stay calm and to trust in You in this situation."

Prayer

Father, when life becomes too much, and when it all becomes overwhelming, help me stay calm and remember You are here with me. Release me into Your peace, never leaving me and never forsaking me. In Jesus' name. Amen.

Your Place of Safety

This I declare about the Lord: He alone is my refuge,
my place of safety; He is my God, and I trust Him.

PSALM 91:2

Where do you feel safe? According to Strong's dictionary, the word refuge means "shelter from rain, storm, danger, and a place of trust." When I find myself feeling the most vulnerable, I know this is the perfect opportunity to resurrect the shelter of trust. That shelter is an opportunity to get cozy next to our big God. Our circumstances during uncertainty can seem larger than life, but building shelters through trusting in Him is how we find our place of safety. The reality is, the rain will happen. The storms will come. But what makes Christian living so different is that we serve a God who controls the storm. Remember the story of Jesus on the boat in the middle of the sea? He was sleeping during the storm. Whenever life gets overwhelming for me, I think about Jesus and how He slept. I want the mind of Christ—to respond not in fear but with trust, and to make my pattern of living one where I know how to seek refuge in the middle of the storm.

That trust includes rest. It includes covering. You may feel exposed, but declare to all your fears who your God is. Speak to the uncertainty with confidence, not doubting, but believing in Him. He knows the way you should go. He also knows the forecast. That is your safe place. It's not in your plans, your analysis, your goals. It's not in your ambitions, your dreams, or your finances. Your place of safety is in the Lord. No matter what happens around you, no matter what falls apart, don't put your hope in circumstances. Put your hope in Christ and find safety on a firm foundation. Even when you don't see the way, KNOW that you are safe in the refuge of the Lord and trust in Him.

Prayer

Father, release me from the bondage of fear and doubt. Help me know that You are there even when I can't see my way, even when the storms of life are raging. Give me such a peace that allows me to have the best sleep of my life. In Jesus' name. Amen.

Sweet Release

For I, the Lord your God, hold your right hand;
it is I who say to you, "Fear not, I am the one who helps you."

ISAIAH 41:13 ESV

Overwhelm has a way of creeping in when we least expect it. You are going about your day, thinking you are being productive, only to look up and feel a weight of heaviness on you. As you look around at the growing to-do list and loads of laundry that seem to never go away, with the needs of your husband and children on your mind, the feelings of overwhelm can become a huge distraction, not only from hearing God but from having the peace of God. God promises that He will help us—just as He was helping the children of Israel in today's verse. He was reassuring them not to panic but to trust in Him. He was saying to them (and to us through this Scripture) that no matter what the circumstances may look like, no matter what is going on around you, no matter what you lost and the things you need, He is the Lord your God.

I invite you to think about your circumstances that seem too big for you to handle. Write down a list of things that bring you stress and anxiety—even when you simply think about them. Make a conscious decision to release them to God. Release the need to get it all done. Release the weight of desire for achievement. We all want to feel productive, but what exactly is realistic for our current season?

You can simply ask God, "What is the priority for today, God? What should I focus on right now?" Everything else can wait. No matter what it looks like, God is here to help you. The key question is, will you allow God to help you?

Prayer

Jesus, I release my will and my future to You.
Thank You for helping me through each step.
I acknowledge You here and now, and I put my trust in You.
In Jesus' name. Amen.

Soar

But those who trust in the Lord will find new strength.
They will soar high on wings like eagles.
They will run and not grow weary.
They will walk and not faint.

ISAIAH 40:31

When I think of a newborn, I think of the ultimate definition of trust. In Merriam-Webster, trust is defined as "assured reliance on the character, ability, strength, or truth of someone or something." Little babies born into an unknown world rely on everyone around them to meet their every need. As they grow and become aware, they either understand it is safe to place their trust in their family or they find out they have very few people who they can trust. Over time, the trust they have in safe places gives way to protective walls.

When we come to learn about Christ, it matters how we process our relationship with Him. He can be the loving Father, even if your earthly father was not so loving. He can be the trusted presence you need to thrive, even if you are used to fighting in a world where abuse, neglect, and abandonment run rampant. Ask God how to release the past, the shame, the guilt, the rejection, the neglect. Whatever it is that is standing in the way of complete trust in God as His child, let's identify it and then make a conscious decision to release it. This walk of intimacy will give you the strength to overcome every barrier that is keeping you from living in complete and total freedom in Christ. As you trust in Him, He will align you with His purpose, allowing you to soar above the clouds and the storm. It is with this reliance on Him that you will gain new sight to see how to run your race without burnout or fainting. Find your area of mistrust, give it to God, and then soar!

Prayer

Father, even when I don't understand why, how, or where, help me trust in You with all things. Release me from any bondage of past relationships that affects how I view You and how I trust in You. Heal every area. In Jesus' name. Amen.

A New Level

Now we see things imperfectly, like puzzling reflections
in a mirror, but then we will see everything with perfect
clarity. All that I know now is partial and incomplete,
but then I will know everything completely,
just as God now knows me completely.

I CORINTHIANS 13:12

Walking through uncertainty is one of the hardest things for anyone to do, but we can be encouraged to know that God is speaking and leading us. It is through prayer, the daily habit of silencing the noise around us, and through worship that He begins to whisper to us concerning the next steps and direction we should take.

Have you ever felt as if you were thrown out of your safety net only to find that it wasn't ever that secure in the first place? Nothing is sure but our faith in Christ. Oftentimes we put our hope in things that we have always known, but when we step out of those places of comfort, we allow God to meet us on a new level of faith. One that we haven't quite experienced yet. We can hold on to the fact that God loves us and knows us. When we rest in this, we realize more each day that the full picture is usually not within our view—only the next step is. If we saw the full picture, faith wouldn't be needed.

Our greatest lesson in this life of faith and purpose is not grounded in reaching our goals or destination. It is grounded in the everyday walk with God. While our vision may blur, allowing God to lead will bring clarity one step at a time. Embrace the partial picture, take the next step of obedience, and allow God to reveal Himself to you each day.

Prayer

Father, release any stubbornness, procrastination, or fear within me that refuses to move forward when I don't see how things will work out. I'm ready to see You more. In Jesus' name. Amen.

Seeking His Face

Don't worry about anything, but in everything,
through prayer and petition with thanksgiving,
present your requests to God.

PHILIPPIANS 4:6 CSB

So often in my own life, my first reaction to a situation has been to gather all the facts, and then make a plan of action. Once I'd made my plan of action, I'd go to God in my daily prayer time and ask Him to bless my plans. If things didn't go my way, I'd find myself confused as to what went wrong. I was left broken and unsure about everything. Then one day God said to me, "You prayed last, not first." It was as if I realized why I had failed the test. In my efforts to fix the situation, I ran ahead of God and asked Him to bless my plans. But Scripture says, "You can make many plans, but the Lord's purpose will prevail" (Proverbs 19:21).

Pray about everything. In order to know the Lord's plans, we must first seek Him before we decide what to do next. This doesn't come naturally to us. Our flesh desires control, and we desire to do things our way. Submitting our mind, will, and emotions—also known as our soul—to God's will requires intention. We must get into the habit of stopping ourselves before we respond to any and every situation. This daily habit can form a new way of thinking and reacting that allows us to seek His face and get clarity and direction before we respond.

God is not a genie who we submit our wishes to and wait for Him to grant them. He is a Father who has a perfect will and plan for our lives. He knows what we can and cannot handle. As a mother, I wouldn't give my three-year-old son—no matter how bad his temper tantrum might be—something that would harm him. Because he's not mature enough to understand why something might hurt him, I allow him to cry through it. Eventually his will gives in and moves on to the next thing. One day when he is older, healthier, and wise, he will realize I was trying to keep him safe. Our Father God has knowledge and understanding of the entire world—the beginning and the end. So when our plans don't go the way we want them to, we must thank God and realize He knows and has our best interest in mind.

Prayer

Father, help me overcome any disappointments when my plans don't go the way I thought they would. Even in my best intentions, I know that I want Your perfect will for my life. I release my will, my plans, my desires into Your hands. In Jesus' name. Amen.

Embrace God's Faithfulness

Don't love money; be satisfied with what you have.
For God has said, "I will never fail you.
I will never abandon you."

HEBREWS 13:5

Many believe the lie that money equals success, power, and purpose. While money is a tool, it is never to be viewed as a god. It's easy to get caught up in the game of wanting more and more, however, if we let this tool become an idol in our lives, we will lose sight of the very Source that brings us true joy.

It's true—the distraction of money can be hard to overcome. However, today's Scripture invites us to embrace God's faithfulness in this area. Repeat the words, "I will never fail you. I will never abandon you," as often as you need, to remind your fears who you serve. When you get into the habit of repeating God's Word out loud, you'll bring every thought and imagination that does not line up with the Word of God under the authority of Christ. Your voice is a powerful tool while you walk through a season of uncertainty. Your words, chosen carefully, give space to faith as it grows within your heart.

Prayer

Father, I release all my resources to You. I give You my time, my money, my energy, my focus. Help me to not idolize money or any resource. You are my God, and I ask that You help me transform my thinking in the area of finances.

In Jesus' name. Amen.

THIS I DECLARE

ABOUT THE LORD:

HE ALONE IS MY REFUGE,

MY PLACE OF SAFETY;

HE IS MY GOD,

AND I TRUST HIM.

Psalm 91:2

Pursuing God

Seek the Kingdom of God above all else,
and live righteously, and He will give you
everything you need.

MATTHEW 6:33

Have you ever been pursued by a love interest in a way that was honoring and respectful? Did it catch you off guard? Being in a relationship with someone who genuinely cares about your dreams and goals is so refreshing.

God desires us to pursue Him with our whole hearts. He not only wants to show us who we are in Him, but He wants us to get to know Him as our creator and our friend. Seeking God is the beginning of this pursuit and being curious about God is the fuel. As we find ourselves hungry to know more, He will reveal more. That revelation is bait to come deeper into the knowledge of who He is and how He functions in our lives.

So, what causes us to not pursue God? Distraction. We fill our calendars with to-dos such as the church bake sale, our kids' choir concert, board meetings, wellness appointments—all of these things are good! But are you finding time to get to know God? What is distracting you today? What has your undivided attention? What habits do you need to break to reset your gaze upon the One who holds your future?

Prayer

Father, I release every distraction that's holding me back from pursuing You and seeking You with all my heart, mind, and soul. In Jesus' name. Amen.

Power over Uncertainty

I will instruct you and teach you in the way you should go;
I will counsel you with my loving eye on you

PSALM 32:8 NIV

Uncertainty is being in a state of doubt. Embracing doubt means that you are willing to move forward with it. You see it as a necessary part of your journey, helping you develop your faith and your relationship with the One who has power over uncertainty. Today, as you go about your tasks, if something is unclear, submit it to God and choose to embrace what you don't know. Remember, God will give the answers when the moment comes to make a decision. He will give you not only the direction for the way you should go but the resources for everything you need as well.

Today's Scripture promises us that He will show us the best path—not the fastest, not the wealthiest, but the best path for our lives. He goes on to promise that He will advise us, which means He will give us information about the journey and will watch over us. Remember, no matter what you are facing, God knows. Because He knows, He has a plan. He is good and His plans are good. We can embrace uncertainty because we can embrace God's goodness in all situations.

Prayer

Father, I'm trying to follow Your path for me.
I get off track sometimes, but I ask You to lead me back
to the road You want me on. Watch over me, my family,
and my future. I embrace Your goodness for us and release all
strongholds and inequities into Your love for me.
In Jesus' name, Amen.

He Knows

Through our union with Christ we too have been claimed
by God as His own inheritance. Before we were even born,
He gave us our destiny; that we would fulfill the plan of God
who always accomplishes every purpose and plan in His heart.

EPHESIANS 1:11 THE PASSION TRANSLATION

Being united with Christ starts in our heart. The place of our belief is the soul of our faith. The unseen world responds to where we put our faith, and our union with Christ allows us to walk in boldness as His sons and daughters. The comforting thing about this journey is that God knows what the end will be. He knows why we were created, and He gave us our destiny before we were formed. While life may feel out of control, God is never out of control. Each moment, He knows. When we change our words from "God, show me how to find my purpose" to "God, show me Your purpose," we position ourselves to see His glory in our lives. That glory is the radiance of His heart through us. When we allow the Son to shine through our lives, we are able to see His hands and His plans.

Have you ever cleaned your entire kitchen only to come back an hour later to see a spot you missed? You think to yourself "How did I miss that?? I thought I cleaned this top to bottom," Could it be that the sun shines in different places through the kitchen window at 8 a.m.

than it does at 2 p.m., so what was hidden in the morning is revealed in the afternoon. Think about it—What areas of your life are unseen because you haven't allowed His light to shine through them? Only when you allow God to shine do the impatient and ambitious sides of your begin to settle, and you can release the "doer" in you and rest in God's plan.

Prayer

Father, shine through my life in ways I have never seen.
Help me stop doing so much and help me rest in You more.
I want Your purpose, not my own. I want Your will,
not my own. I want Your plans, not my own.
In Jesus' name. Amen.

True Delight, True Connection

*Trust in the Lord and do good. Then you will live safely in the
land and prosper. Take delight in the Lord, and He will give you
your heart's desires.*

PSALM 37:3–4

The definition of the word delight is "to take pleasure in." When
we take pleasure in something, we enjoy it. We can't wait to do
it again. What are some things in your life that you enjoy? Do you
take delight in planning fun family outings, exploring new restaurants,
or traveling to fun destinations? Or experiencing new adventures with
the people you love. Or do you enjoy having deep conversations that
explore complex topics?

Today's Scripture passage directs us to have hope that God wants
to give us our heart's desires. We can stand on this promise with surety.
However, He's also desiring us to take delight in Him first. The goal is
for our hearts to be aligned with His. When we want what God wants
for us, we are grounded in His larger purpose for our lives. It takes
intention to delight yourself in the Lord. Once you spend time with
Him consistently, having a daily conversation with Him, even hourly
conversations with Him, allowing Him to show Himself to you in
greater ways, then you will start looking forward to your time with Him.

This adventure with God is both exciting and uplifting. It is through our faith and trust in Him that we feed on the joy that comes through His plans. As a good Father, He longs to give us gifts. He also longs to spend time with us so we can grow and develop and shed every negative thought spoken over us. He wants to heal our hearts, focus our ambitions, and release His glory over us in ways we could never imagine. That positioning is through relationship and connection. Through the good and the challenging moments, through our failures, mistakes, and doubts, He wants to walk with us, teaching us His ways over our own.

Prayer

Father, each and every day, show me how to delight in You.
As I walk through my day today, speak with me.
I release every desire in my heart that does not
align itself with You. In Jesus' name. Amen.

Embrace His Next Steps for You

The heart of man plans his way,
but the Lord establishes his steps.

PROVERBS 16:9 ESV

One of the most frustrating things at times is trying to force something to happen in our lives that is not a part of God's purpose for us. Have you ever had a dream that didn't come true? Maybe you wanted to be a professional singer but your vocal cords just didn't cooperate. Or maybe you wanted to be a broadcast journalist giving the evening news, but you ended up living in a rural area with no tv station in miles. Whatever your plan may have been, it just didn't happen that way. Have you ever thought that maybe that dream was not meant to be a part of your journey?

And then there's times when you focus on your gifts, stop trying to force things to happen, and you start to see God's purpose. Did it feel good to let the idea of singing go? Not at first, but once you embraced the things God gave you, you realized that your journey was just as beautiful and impactful. When you surrender your will and embrace who He created you to be, you saw yourself from His perspective and no longer desired other gifts.

Is it time to think about the areas of your life that you have planned? It's not easy to lay down your plans for God's steps. He often gives us the next step, not the whole plan. But His steps are certain

and will never fail us. His steps take our gifts into account. His steps bring us into alignment with His great plan for our lives. His steps help build our character and integrity and uproot any motives that are not pure within our hearts. He loves us enough to not overwhelm us with the larger plan but graces us with the direction on what to do next. His joy is contagious when we allow ourselves the opportunity to commune with Him every day, never taking for granted that He is speaking to us and through us.

Prayer

Father, I release my plans to You, and I embrace Your steps for me. Show me the next step to take. In Jesus' name. Amen.

Casting Mountains

I tell you the truth, you can say to this mountain,
"May you be lifted up and thrown into the sea,"
and it will happen. But you must really believe it
will happen and have no doubt in your heart.

MARK 11:23

Imagine you are taking a long walk to get from one city to another. As you start off on your journey, you run into a large mountain. The thing about this mountain is that to get on the other side of it will require you to go through a dangerous pathway that could be life-threatening. There is no way to get to your destination except by way of this mountain.

Mountains represent barriers in our lives that prevent us from forward movement. They can be many things, such as a wrong thought pattern, generational issues within our family, a way of living that doesn't embrace God's love, abuse, fear, doubt, unbelief, and so much more. When you make the decision to live a God-purposed life, there will be mountains that come up on your journey—fears you must overcome and situations that seem to be standing in your way.

God gives us victory over these mountains, and it's important to understand the power of our own words as well. Today's Scripture verse advises us to speak to these mountains. It's not enough to just hope in your heart. You must use the most powerful part of who God created you to be, and that is your voice. Out loud, in prayer, truly believing what you are saying. Identify your mountain and command it to be cast into the sea. God promises us that it will happen. The only stipulation God gives is that we must really believe it and have no doubt in our hearts. The question you need to ask yourself is, "Do I really believe without doubt?"

Prayer

Father, help me believe without any doubt in my heart. I release the mountain standing in my way, and I cast it into the sea. In Jesus' name. Amen.

Freedom in Forgiveness

I tell you, you can pray for anything, and if you believe that
you've received it, it will be yours. But when you are praying,
first forgive anyone you are holding a grudge against,
so that your Father in heaven will forgive your sins, too.

MARK 11:24–25

Forgiveness is not always an easy topic to cover in relation to embracing the plan God has for our lives. This journey of forgiveness can be challenging or untroubling, depending on what or who it is that you are faced with forgiving. Imagine for a moment standing on the bank of a river. You need to get across to the other side, but there are no boats around. Now imagine you are walking up and down the bank of the river and you run into a man who has a boat and agrees to take you across the river to get you to your destination. The boat represents forgiveness; the man represents Jesus. The river represents the issue that needs your forgiveness. God knows how difficult it can be for us to forgive, but He is able to journey with us through the process of forgiveness. If we don't forgive, this issue stands in our way of getting to where God is trying to take us. He is telling us that we must first forgive to get to the other side of the issue.

If you are praying and believing God for something and you seem to not be getting an answer, think about any areas of unforgiveness that you need to address. Is there someone who you are holding something against? Have you been trying to justify why you will never be able to forgive someone who hurt you deeply? I'm not saying you should welcome them back into your life or even have a relationship with them. Why not take this to God in prayer? Ask Him the best way to free your heart from the pain, and then lean into Him as He carries you over the water.

Prayer

God, I acknowledge my humanity in this moment,
but most importantly, I acknowledge Your power.
I release every person I am holding unforgiveness against, and
today, I forgive all of them. Help me to fully forgive,
even if it takes more than one moment or one day.
In Jesus' name. Amen.

Taste and See

*This Book of the Law shall not depart from your mouth,
but you shall meditate on it day and night, so that you
may be careful to do according to all that is written in it.
For then you will make your way prosperous, and then you
will have good success. Have I not commanded you?
Be strong and courageous. Do not be frightened,
and do not be dismayed, for the Lord your God
is with you wherever you go.*

JOSHUA 1:8–9 ESV

Success is predictable. That is a strong statement to make, but it is true. God, in His power and wisdom, gave us the formula to be successful in life and in all that we do. When uncertainty comes, we can stand on the Word of God. Today's Scripture is just one of many principles that God has shared with us about living a successful life. So what does it look like to meditate on the Word of God day and night? It looks like reading the Word of God, asking God for deeper understanding of it, and allowing it to get deep into our hearts to a point that we receive transformation and revelation from it. So why not make it habit to read at least a chapter a day out of the Bible, just like taking vitamins or brushing our teeth?

Ask God deeper questions about the Bible verses throughout the day and keep the conversation going as if you're speaking with a friend. While some may not understand why reading the Bible daily is so important, God summons us to try Him, to taste and see that the Lord is good. When we read the Bible and allow it to read us, the very core of our heart is changed. We can be assured that our desires and hopes come into alignment with God's as we allow His Word to penetrate our souls, redirect our lives, and show us what kingdom success actually looks like.

Prayer

Father, help me release anything on my plate that is taking away from the time I need to read Your Word and meditate on it day and night. Help me fall in love with Your Word again. Give me such a hunger that I look forward to talking to You every day. In Jesus' name. Amen.

God Fulfills His Promises

*Not a single one of all the good promises the Lord
had given to the family of Israel was left unfulfilled;
everything He had spoken came true.*

JOSHUA 21:45

During the holiday season, my kids love to tell my husband and me what they want for Christmas. They don't know if we will get it for them, but that doesn't stop them from asking us. This is an example of the foundation of hope. It's the ability to ask, not knowing the end result but knowing the provider can make it happen. This concept is clear in the area of faith. It is even more clear in the promises of God throughout the Bible. One thing we can rest in is that God will fulfill His promises. Some of the promises are unconditional. They will happen no matter what we do. God's love is an example of this. His grace, which is unearned favor, is another example.

As you walk through this season of uncertainty, remember God's promises. Write them down. Someone once said that when you read the Word of God, do it with intentionality. Highlight the promises of God. Mark them to help when you get to a place where you need to be reminded of what God says about your situation. He does His best work in the middle of our faith. At times, it seems like He doesn't see us, hear us, or work on our behalf, but that is where we activate our faith and our ask. We find the promises in Scripture and speak them back to our Father.

This season, you may not see the way, you may not understand what is happening, but know that it is in the unseen that your faith is growing the most. Embracing uncertainty is about embracing the foundation of faith. It is about embracing trust, and this is where you grow roots down into His Word. This place you're in is the ground of your next level. A level built on God's Word and faith can withstand the weight of the issues and circumstances of life. It can withstand God's purpose for and His promises over your life.

Prayer

Father, thank You for Your many promises. If I have said or done anything that has stopped the flow of blessings over my life, I repent. Help me know and embrace Your perfect will and Your promises for me. In Jesus' name. Amen.

How to Fly

The Lord directs the steps of the godly. He delights in every detail of their lives. Though they stumble, they will never fall, for the Lord holds them by the hand.

PSALM 37:23–24

"God, I feel like I'm falling." This was the exact statement I made to God during a season in my life after I had stepped out in faith. The uncertainty was like gravity pulling me down, allowing fear to grip my heart, mind, and focus. I was having a very difficult time with the new normal of walking by faith, without any control or something solid to hold on to. Truth is, all my life has been a walk of faith. Even with a "normal" job, even thinking I knew what should or would happen, it was all suspended in the love and power of God—that at any moment, life could change.

Once I stepped out to be home with my children, giving up the security of a job and not knowing what the future would hold for us, this feeling of falling was very prevalent. It was today's Scripture passage that reminded me that God would not let me fall. Not only did the timing of me coming home matter, but it also needed to happen to prepare me one year in advance before the world would change forever with a pandemic. The world was thrown into a season of uncertainty in March 2020, and I had already been living it.

So when God says that He delights in every detail of our lives, believe it. For me, I stumbled into trusting Him. I wish I could say it was an easy transition. It wasn't. It was messy and hard, and the uncertainty was overwhelming. As someone who has gone through it, I assure you that God will not let you fall. If you're like me and you are feeling the weight of uncertainty, let go and fall into His hands, His will, and His trust. The falling is how you learn to trust, just as a baby eagle learns to fly. The mother eagle pushes it out of the nest. Your wings must learn to spread as you feel the pull of uncertainty. You won't always feel this way. It will get easier. You've been flying and trusting God in one area or another most of your life, but now your altitude has gotten higher, and it may require learning how to fly all over again. You got this.

Prayer

Father, I release this fear of falling, this fear of failing, and this weight of doubt into Your trust. I know You love me, and I know You won't let me fall. Thank You for being a loving Father. In Jesus' name. Amen.

BUT THOSE WHO
TRUST IN THE LORD
WILL FIND NEW STRENGTH.
THEY WILL SOAR HIGH
ON WINGS LIKE EAGLES.
THEY WILL RUN AND
NOT GROW WEARY.
THEY WILL WALK
AND NOT FAINT.

Isaiah 40:31

Confidence or Pride

Don't be wise in your own eyes; fear the Lord and turn away from evil. This will be healing for your body and strengthening for your bones.

PROVERBS 3:7–8 CSB

In today's verse, God is saying not to think too highly of yourself or be impressed with your wisdom. And then the healing process for your body will begin, giving strength to your bones.

Stress has scientifically proven to undermine our physical and mental health. I have learned that many people get pride and confidence mixed up. They believe that speaking highly of themselves and putting themselves on a pedestal is having confidence when it really only reveals a prideful heart. However, God is instructing us to humble ourselves by putting our confidence in Him. And when we do this, our humility gives space for the glory of God to be revealed over and over in our lives. When our ego fills the room, where does God's glory reside?

Fearing the Lord means to be in reverent awe of His holiness, and to honor Him as the God of great glory, majesty, purity and power. Our confidence is in His ability to do great things through us. Our confidence comes from knowing where our help comes from. We lean on, rely on, and trust in God in every area of our lives. That confidence, at the core, comes from ability—not our own ability but the very essence, direction, and guidance of God.

Prayer

Father, I release all pride out of my heart, soul, and mind. I surrender this area to You. Even when I have good intentions, show me myself and any pride that I am walking in, and then change me, God. Teach me Your ways so I can fear You and turn away from any and all evil. In Jesus' name. Amen.

From Uncertainty to Faith

Trust in the Lord with all your heart;
do not depend on your own understanding.
Seek His will in all you do,
and He will show you which path to take.

PROVERBS 3:5–6

Uncertainty can be paralyzing. It can leave you feeling stuck and unsure of which direction to go. Uncertainty is defined as a feeling or attitude that one does not know the truth, truthfulness, or trustworthiness of someone or something. Paired with uncertainty is oftentimes the feeling of being uncomfortable. One day, I sat in my car thinking about the unknown future. I had just left a powerful small group of moms who prayed with me. As I sat in the car, I felt God in all the fullness of who He is—a comforting Father. Just as a father provides, protects, and guides his children, I felt His love so strongly in that moment. I knew from that moment forward that even though I didn't have the details, I had the heart of the One who knows all, sees all, has all power in His hands, and is everywhere at all times.

I wish I could say I immediately felt the uncertainty leave, but I didn't. Instead, I felt an immeasurable amount of peace amid the uncertainty. I just knew everything would be fine. Over time, as God and His faithfulness became evident each day, I began to walk with confidence, knowing that my process had evolved from uncertainty to faith. From faith, I developed an intimacy with God and His Word. I found myself in Scripture, learning through the lives of those who also walked in faith on the water of uncertainty.

Is it time for you to sit in His presence and find His peace in the face of your uncertainty? Maybe it's time to find a small group or join an online Bible study. Pray and ask God to lead you into a deeper faith, and then follow His lead.

Prayer

Father, this is not easy, but I know You love me.
Help me receive this love and release every barrier keeping
me from evolving toward a greater depth of faith in You.
I'm ready to embrace the uncertainty of this season.
Thank You for never failing me, even when I don't understand.
I trust You, God. Let's do this. In Jesus' name. Amen.

Embracing Peace

I am leaving you with a gift—peace of mind and heart.
And the peace I give is a gift the world cannot give.
So don't be troubled or afraid.

JOHN 14:27

This earthly life that God has allowed us all to experience has many reminders that we are so very human. In one moment we can be riding high, and the next moment we can be captivated by debilitating fear, unable to move forward. When I find myself sitting in vulnerability and all the emotions that come with it, I have learned to say, "God, this is hard, and this hurts, but I trust You."

In the thick of that prayer, with my eyes closed, I receive the gift of peace of mind and heart. Peace of mind is the realization that I have come to the end of my doing, my understanding, and my wisdom. Peace of mind shuts down the voices of how and why and embraces the substance of things hoped for—faith.

Peace of heart deals with the core of my desires, hopes, and dreams. It is where God tells the storm to be still. It is the place where He shows up in the middle of the water and invites me to walk with Him through what looks impossible. Through His love, this gift is given, but it is through our faith and trust that we take on the responsibility of receiving the gift.

Embracing peace while staring at vulnerability gives you power through renewed confidence in who God is and the power He has over every storm.

Prayer

Father, I receive the peace of mind and heart that You have gifted to me. I release all anxiety, depression, unbelief, fear, and doubt. I embrace peace, and I ask You to calm the storms in my mind and my heart. In Jesus' name. Amen.

Grow Your Roots

Rooted and built up in Him, strengthened in the faith
as you were taught, and overflowing with thankfulness.

COLOSSIANS 2:7 NIV

Have you ever planted a garden? Every year, right around March, I start tilling the ground of my garden, getting it ready to receive the seeds I want to plant. I usually choose the plant I want to grow based on how it will behave in the garden. Cucumbers have a small seed, but in my first year of gardening, I learned that once the seed's roots grow down into the soil, the result is quite large, and it produces a long stem and many cucumbers. That year, I only planted four small seeds, but I got more than thirty cucumbers. I also ended up with an unexpectedly large and long plant that wrapped itself around the other plants in the square garden. The cucumber plant was designed—not by me and not by the surroundings I put it in, but by its DNA—to overflow where it is planted.

We are created in the image and likeness of a BIG God, and if we allow our roots to grow down into Him by reading, studying, and meditating on God's Word, our faith will grow stronger than we ever knew possible. In this season of vulnerability, it is the perfect time to lean into God, ask Him for guidance, and focus on His Word. And when you do, your stem will grow long and your leaves will be large, able to receive from the Son all the nutrients He provides.

I used to read a statement such as today's verse from Scripture and think it sounded good, but it wasn't until I experienced it for myself that I realized how powerful it is and how it can literally transform an entire life. Will you allow God to help you grow in your faith, bringing you to a place that overflows with thankfulness? That is a place of surrender. It is making the decision every day to get into the presence of God and seek Him with all your heart, mind, and soul. Everything that's planted in your life can grow in the soil, which is the very presence of God, with the help of water, which is His Word, and in the warmth of the sun, which is the Holy Spirit. Get planted and then get rooted.

Prayer

Father, help me get planted. I release all stubbornnes and
fear of being planted. Help me find the soil You want me in.
I'm ready to grow deeper in You, to know You more,
and to allow who You are to enrich and grow my faith
in the truth I will be taught. In Jesus' name. Amen.

Breaking the Mental Barrier

Don't be afraid, for I am with you. Don't be discouraged,
for I am your God. I will strengthen you and help you.
I will hold you up with My victorious right hand.

ISAIAH 41:10

It was a cool spring morning when I woke up to participate in my first triathlon. I had trained for three months before the event. At the start of training, I didn't know how to swim very well, but thankfully, I have always been up for a challenge. Over the course of training, I got the hang of swimming, but I knew swimming a half mile across a lake would take great courage.

On the day before the triathlon, I got into the lake for a practice swim. I had never swum across a lake, but again, I was up for the challenge. I got into the water and started swimming. As soon as my body passed the line showing the drop-off, meaning the water was now very deep and at a level where I was unable to stand up, every muscle in my body began to cramp. I turned back and quickly got to shore. I thought to myself, Wow, that hurt, but let's try it again. Like before, every muscle tensed up and I had to return to shore.

That night, I prayed to God for help. Fear overwhelmed me, and I was unsure if I could cross this lake. God gave me the idea to sing a worship song in rhythm to the strokes. I could envision myself swimming and singing across the lake. Peace came over me, and the next day I was ready to swim. I got in the water, focused my eyes on the sun reflecting on the water, and started singing at the rhythm of my swim strokes. I didn't focus on when or where the drop-off was, I just continued to swim until I got to the other side.

Fear has a way of making us feel paralyzed, and then discouragement sets in making it that much harder to walk by faith. Yet when we ask, God will give us specific directions on not only how to move forward but ways to reduce our anxiety and fear. He cares about us and every detail of our lives. I broke through a mental barrier of fear that day. Now I know that with God on my side, I can look fear in the eye and worship my Savior as I walk forward.

Prayer

I release all fear and discouragement from my mind, heart, and soul. God, I ask that You give me specific directions on how to make the next step. I believe today's Scripture verse is true, and I believe in You. In Jesus' name. Amen.

Trust and Rest

I cried out, "I am slipping!" but Your unfailing love, O Lord, supported me. When doubts filled my mind, Your comfort gave me renewed hope and cheer.

PSALM 94:18–19

To celebrate my husband's birthday, I surprised him with a trip to try indoor skydiving. I had never done it, but we both love doing new things, and I thought this would be the perfect way to celebrate him. As we arrived at the location, we were given training to know what we needed to do while inside the shoot. The shoot was basically a large clear tunnel with a really big fan blowing us up through it. One of the directions we were given was to keep our bodies straight with hands and legs extended out. The facilitators would be responsible for making us go up and down; we were to only keep our bodies straight.

Once I got in, I was surprised at how fear immediately came over me when I was no longer on the ground. My hope and life for that moment were in the hands of my instructor. We got up and down, back up and back down, in the huge clear tube. I remember being so stiff because I didn't want to do anything I wasn't supposed to do. In the moment, I tried to enjoy myself, but it was hard because I was completely outside my comfort zone. I was no longer in control of anything.

Thankfully, I landed safely and went out for the next person to come in. As I sat there, I thought to myself, Wow, that was fun. What was I so scared of? These guys are experts, and there are tons of safety measures in place to keep us all safe. Yet as I flew up and down, I could only focus on if my body was stiff enough. The second time around, I made it a priority to enjoy it. Yes, I still felt very uncomfortable, but the experience was finally appreciated as something I will never forget.

How often do we get to places in our lives, as we set out to do what we believe God has called us to do, only to feel like we are in too deep? The thoughts of doubt fill our minds as life seems to be consuming us on all sides. Just as my facilitator was there the whole time, holding on to the strap making me go up and down, Jesus is always there and in control of our lives as well. When we trust that He is there, we can finally rest in that fact and try to embrace the journey and see the hope and cheer in it all.

Prayer

Father, thank You for always being there for me.
I release my worries and concerns into Your care.
I embrace hope and joy as I walk forward in Your will
for my life. In Jesus' name. Amen.

Staying Afloat

Christ may dwell in your hearts through faith—that you,
being rooted and grounded in love.

EPHESIANS 3:17 ESV

Lily pads are fascinating, aren't they? Their leaves seemingly float on water. They are flat in nature, and many times we see lake frogs sitting on them. They come in all sizes. Some are as small as the palm of our hands, while others are large enough for people to sit on! The largest ones are usually found in the Amazon basin, but the most fascinating thing about them is that while they look like they are floating, underneath is a stem and tons of roots holding each one up and supplying nutrients. The roots go down deep into the water, and that is how the lily pads survive and stay afloat. If you remove them from the water, they will disconnect from the roots that provide life and keep them strong.

Isn't this similar to our lives? Many of us are raised to look at our own efforts and intellect as the answer to our questions. It may seem that we are floating through life by our own efforts, but when we disconnect from the One who is providing for us, at first we may survive, but over time our lives begin to disintegrate, as we are no longer connected to the source of life itself.

The roots of the large lily pads are very strong. They are not flimsy, because whatever sits on the lily pads must be sustained by the strength of the roots underneath. As our roots grow down deep into God's love, they strengthen to be able to handle whatever life "sits" on us. When you allow Christ to make His home in your heart and you trust in Him, you grow your roots down into Him. When you decide to live for Him, to seek Him every single day, you are allowing those very roots to keep you strong.

Prayer

Father, please release my roots from unimportant things, and I redirect my focus on You. I welcome You into my heart and ask that You make Your home there.
In Jesus' name. Amen.

Alignment

So be strong and courageous! Do not be afraid and do not panic before them. For the Lord your God will personally go ahead of you. He will neither fail you nor abandon you.

DEUTERONOMY 31:6

The word fear, which in Hebrew is yirah, occurs more than 318 times in the Bible. It's clear God knew that one of the greatest things we would need to overcome is fear. Fear tries to prevent the movement of faith in the lives of believers. Consuming the Word of God restructures our thoughts and brings our minds into alignment with God's perspective rather than letting them settle on what others tell us, what our situation is revealing to us, or what we currently think. He sees all and knows all. He is in complete control. He has a perfect will and plan for our lives.

This alignment requires us to submit and lay down our own thoughts and beliefs and embrace His Word. It is through eyes of faith that we retrain ourselves to walk, believe, endure, and be guided. And while we know that going from faith to faith and glory to glory is not a straight line going up. At times, our season of pruning or rest will look like things have slowed down, but through it all, God is still being glorified and we are still rising.

Many get lost in this moment, believing they are doing something wrong. While that may be true in some situations, we must allow God to speak to us through His Word and give us direction and understanding for our current situation. I've learned to be grateful for the pruning seasons. It is in these moments that I look fear in the eyes and continue to choose Jesus. As I continue to choose faith, my endurance grows, my patience grows, and my desires change. It's a refining place and a necessary place.

Prayer

Father, help me be courageous. This season of vulnerability has exposed all my fears. I ask that You release anything preventing me from embracing this season.
In Jesus' name. Amen.

Tough Love

*Who is this that obscures My plans
with words without knowledge?*

JOB 38:2 NIV

Whenever you are facing an insurmountable situation or even if you just want to remind yourself of who your God is, read chapter 38 of the book of Job. Job had many questions after God allowed the devil to test him. Many of Job's questions were understandable given his circumstances. (He lost just about everything and was barely hanging on to his life.) In the account, it is God's response to Job that always shakes me to my core. He says, "Where were you when I laid the foundations of the earth?" (38:4), and "Have you ever commanded the morning to appear and caused the dawn to rise in the east?" (38:12). God was speaking to every doubtful thought of Job's, giving him the tough love he needed to endure it all.

I love how this story resonates on such a deep level when we face much less hardship than Job did. It is in God's faithfulness that we rest our thoughts. His answers challenge the concepts of our world and the things we don't think about every day. Most of us don't think about the sun and if it will ever fall out of the sky. Most of us go to beaches without the fear that the water will suddenly overwhelm us on the shore. We rely on God's faithfulness even when we don't always remember or acknowledge it. Shift your focus and see all around you how God is holding every piece of your life together.

Prayer

Father, You are awesome in all Your ways.
There is none like You. I release this heavy worry
and difficult situation to You. Give me Your perspective,
that I may see clearly. In Jesus' name. Amen.

Angels Among Us

For He will order His angels to protect you wherever you go.

PSALM 91:11

My journey to know the Lord began at a mall. A small-statured older woman with silver-gray hair walked up to my mom and me. She told us about a church and advised us to worship God with everything in us. My mom happened to be looking for a church, and when we visited, she gave her life to God. Soon after, we joined the church. I was eleven years old, and while it took me a few months, I eventually gave my life to the Lord too.

The church was not very big, and everyone knew each another. We asked around to find the older woman, and no one knew who we were talking about. We continued searching for years and asked everyone in the church, but no one knew her or had ever met her. She would have been easily noticeable at this church, so we concluded that she was an angel. Our encounter changed the course of our family's life. We can retrace our life-changing moment to that conversation in the mall. I am humbled at the idea that I might have had an interaction with an real angel.

Truth is, angels are ministering spirits sent to serve those who will inherit salvation (Hebrews 1:14). Scripture also tells us that angels can appear to us as strangers, like the woman did (Hebrews 13:2). We didn't have to stop and talk to the woman at the mall. We could have kept walking. I truly believe that God planned this divine moment for me and my family, and I'm forever thankful. Have you ever had a moment like this? Take some time to reflect on it today and be sure to let God know how thankful you are that He is still protecting and loving you—even in these times.

Prayer

Father, open my eyes to see You moving around me.
Help me know that there are angels all around, protecting me.
Release me from the me that is too proud to see You.
In Jesus' name. Amen.

I WILL INSTRUCT YOU

AND TEACH YOU

IN THE WAY

YOU SHOULD GO;

I WILL COUNSEL YOU

WITH MY LOVING EYE

ON YOU.

Psalm 32:8 NIV

Choose Patience

Be completely humble and gentle; be patient,
bearing with one another in love.

EPHESIANS 4:2 NIV

Some people are naturally calm. No matter the situation, they have a response of calm and peace. Humility is not a person's demeanor. It is the position of their heart. It is at the core of their motives, values, and ethics. It is what we must train ourselves to do while seeking directions and wisdom from God. Being humble and gentle allows us to take a moment to step back and think about what's going on and how we can give a godly response to a situation.

Truth is, people are going to do things that don't make us feel good. They will make mistakes, have bad motives, and struggle in different areas of their lives. The question is will we be able to be patient with them. When we meet someone, we need to start the relationship with the idea that they may not always make you feel the best. There will likely be disagreements and misunderstandings. We are all a work in progress. This is why we must make room for their faults.

God did not design us to live and do life alone. Community is one of the first things Jesus created with His disciples. They all had issues and various viewpoints, yet God still chose them. He knew their flaws. He was patient with them. They became part of a bigger plan—one that used their flaws and strengths to reach the overall goal. We can't dismiss people because they are flawed. Instead, let's ask God for wisdom in these moments. Remember that the grace we ask for from others in dealing with our flaws is what we must give to them as well.

Prayer

Father, help me be humble and gentle.

Increase my capacity in the area of patience.

Help me seek You for wisdom in dealing with Your children.

Help me love them like You love them.

I release all grudges I am holding against anyone.

In Jesus' name. Amen.

Countercultural

You will show me the way of life, granting me the joy of Your presence and the pleasures of living with You forever.

PSALM 16:11

Our experience of life with Christ will require constant reprogramming. Why? Because our culture and society are embedding their thoughts and beliefs into our everyday lives. In the middle of summer, a retail store has back-to-school items placed at the front of the store. A few months later, it has fall and Thanksgiving decor, then Christmas, New Year's, and Valentine's. When you look up, reminders of what we SHOULD be planning or talking about are all around us. It is as if someone else is leading and guiding our decisions. This happens so frequently and covertly that no one ever challenges it. Most of us don't mind the reminders, but on a deeper level, what else are we being taught? What thought patterns do we need to uproot?

The Word of God and His presence are our answers. Today's verse from Scripture reminds us that God will show us the way of life. When we seek His face and allow Him to direct our ways, we will enjoy the joy of His presence and the pleasures of living with Him forever. God has so many promises for us in the Bible. Your challenge today is to find two promises of God that you can hold on to over the next month. Allow God to reveal Himself to you through these promises.

Also, find ways of your thinking and living that are contrary to God's Word. How can you adjust your life to align with His ways and His thoughts? Being countercultural gives you an opportunity to live according to God's plan, and it will also help you walk through seasons of uncertainty and vulnerability with a foundation of faith in Christ. This foundation is not shaky, and you can be sure that God will meet your every need. He already knows what your needs are, and if He clothes and feeds the birds of the air, how much more will He do for you? Trust Him.

Prayer

Father, help me release cultural mindsets and ways of living that do not line up with Your Word. Teach me Your ways. In Jesus' name. Amen.

Playing By the Rules

Jesus replied, "I assure you, no one can enter the Kingdom of God without being born of water and the Spirit. Humans can reproduce only human life, but the Holy Spirit gives birth to spiritual life."

JOHN 3:5–6

When I was learning how to swim, I felt like there were new rules I had to learn. Being in the water was not like being on land. The pull of gravity on land is very evident, and our world is shaped in the constraints of this force. In water, however, some people can do things that defy gravity. The law of gravity says that what goes up MUST come down. This also applies in water, except for those who understand the new rules in water AND have the physical body that supports them.

For instance, when I allowed my body to go flat, I would float. When I stretched my hands out front, my feet back kicking, and my arms pulling the water, making me horizontal with the water, I began to float without much effort. I had to trust the water and embrace sinking just a bit until the floating started. The moment I tensed up or started to get afraid, I found myself sinking.

This same principle applies to the kingdom of God. There are rules in God's kingdom, and His Word is the most powerful source in it.

When we respond to God's love with obedience to these rules, we begin to experience the beauty of His Word. And then we get to live a life that is not bound by worldly intellect and sometimes even defies all logic.

We've all heard the biblical principle "what you sow, you will also reap." For example, the seed of man produces another human, but God produces the life of His Spirit in us. Sow in the Spirit so you may also reap in the Spirit. Take time today to engage with the Holy Spirit, allowing Him to share with you the principles of the kingdom and what a successful life looks like to God.

Prayer

Father, help me learn the principles of Your kingdom.
Help me release the tensions of life and to learn how
to sense the nudges from Your Spirit. In Jesus' name. Amen.

Love, Grace, and Mercy

But God, being rich in mercy,
because of the great love with which he loved us,
even when we were dead in our trespasses,
made us alive together with Christ—
by grace you have been saved.

EPHESIANS 2:4–5 ESV

Rich in mercy." Mercy is defined as judgment withheld. God, in His love for us, has not only given us the option to choose Jesus and His ways but also been merciful to us when we haven't chosen Jesus' ways. I cringe thinking about all the times I got things wrong and what my life would look like outside of God's mercy. I'm thankful for God's mercy because it allows me to learn, adjust, and grow.

The key thing we must realize is God's mercy is the padding for when we fall. God's love is beyond comprehension—when you look at His grace and mercy, you see a love that doesn't make much sense. God gave his ONLY Son, Jesus Christ, to die for us so that we might live and have eternal life. That realization is transformational. He believes in us and is rooting for us, like a father rooting for his son during football practice or like a mother getting excited when her child learns to read.

Parenting has given me a deeper perspective into God and His kingdom like no other thing has ever done. There is something about having your own children and sacrificing for them that gives you a glimpse of the gravity of what God went through when Jesus died for our sins. This love, along with the grace, which is unmerited (unearned) favor, is how we come into the knowledge and relationship with Jesus Christ. Our belief, hope, faith, and trust in Him is how we receive salvation. The journey of renewing our mind happens over time and throughout our daily conversation with God. Embracing vulnerability is about allowing God to give you the love, grace, and mercy you need to not only survive but thrive in this season.

Prayer

Father, I receive Your love, grace, and mercy into my heart.
Thank You for being so faithful in every season of my life.
From this moment forward, I want to know You more.
I release all guilt and shame that I've carried because
of my poor decisions. In Jesus' name. Amen.

Overcoming Distractions

*See, I am sending an angel before you to protect you
on your journey and lead you safely to the place
I have prepared for you.*

EXODUS 23:20

At the end of my time in college, I had the opportunity to study abroad. I went to prep sessions my school offered to help me understand this third-world country I would visit. I learned what I should and should not do while I was there. I was excited to travel because this was a place I had never visited, and I didn't know what to expect while there. All I did know was that my professors had made this trip in previous semesters with different students and the reviews were awesome. I never questioned if the journey would be amazing. I knew I would always remember it and cherish the memories we created.

The thing that gave me the most peace was knowing my professors had gone before me. While I had no idea what to expect, they did. They also tried their best to prepare me for the journey, reassuring me that everything would be fine. The Lord does the same for us. He sends angels into our lives to protect us on our journey. These angels are assigned to the safety of (Enter your name here). Their job is to lead you to a place of safety. Your job is to be in alignment and undistracted so that you can listen and hear.

When I think about the greatest challenge of our generation, it is that we are so very distracted. From our phones and the next Netflix series to all the online engagement opportunities, when do we have time to quiet the noise and hear God? Now is the time to remove distraction. The road ahead is uncertain to us, but God is never out of control.

Prayer

Father, I put my trust in You as I go on this journey. I release all the distractions and noises around me. Help me restructure my life so that I will have time to commune with You. In Jesus' name. Amen.

Flying Fearless

King David said this about Him: 'I see that the Lord is always with me. I will not be shaken, for He is right beside me.

ACTS 2:25

I'm not a fan of flying in an airplane. I will do it to get to my destination, but it is definitely not my favorite thing to do. I do, however, love traveling, and one year my family went on a trip to New York City. The journey was a three-hour flight from Dallas to New York. Once in the air, turbulence started and I began to have a panic attack. I've learned how to manage panic attacks, so no one else knew I was having it. When I felt like I was going to fall through the plane—the worst feeling in the world—I prayed and asked God to help me. I focused on His love for me, and I envisioned a place like a garden that I could relax in. I also remembered verses from Scripture to reassure me of God's protection and His promises. Slowly the attack ceased, and I was able to endure the rest of the flight without too much emotional turmoil.

Over time, I changed my response to these attacks. Instead of allowing them to consume me, I now meet them at the door with the Word of God. I don't know why God has blessed me in this way, but I truly believe God has delivered me from panic attacks. Today's Scripture verse is a great example of what I think about when I'm afraid, when I experience anxiety, or when any attack tries to consume my mental and emotional space. This is also the verse I speak when I

sense physical danger around me or my family. I will not be shaken! Remember this wherever you go. Mark this page and gather ten more verses to hold on to. Use them like the stones David used when he faced Goliath. He wasn't concerned about how big Goliath was or how many stones he needed to kill him. He knew God would be victorious. Your fears will try to shake your world. Remind them of how big your God is and keep on going.

Prayer

Father, help me remember that I will not be shaken.
Direct me to the Scriptures that give me strength
and remind me of Your protection when I need it the most.
I release all anxiety and panic in any situation, and I lay down
every burden at Your feet. In Jesus' name. Amen.

Light in the Darkness

Lord, you light my lamp; my God illuminates my darkness.
With you I can attack a barricade, and with my God
I can leap over a wall.

PSALM 18:28–29 CSB

Are you facing a wall today? Or maybe you've scaled a few walls in your day. My wall was infertility. When I was diagnosed with having a prolactinoma, a noncancerous tumor of the pituitary gland, I didn't think too much of it because I was single at the time. Starting a family was the furthest thing from my mind. A few months later I met the man who is now my husband, and a few years into our marriage I realized my diagnosis was an issue. We went to see a fertility doctor and were told that I had not only a prolactinoma that caused infertility but also polycystic ovary syndrome (PCOS), which is the leading cause of infertility in women.

As I sat in the doctor's office staring at my huge wall of infertility, I could only rely on the little bit of faith I had and the great faith my husband had. I had to go into a special time of praying and fasting. It was during this season that I saw God's light in the midst of my darkness. My hope came in the form of testimonies from others who were on the other side of experiencing the faithfulness of God. My light also came through the Word of God as I spoke it over myself. I came to a place of complete surrender—wanting not my will but His to be done.

On one difficult day, as I walked away from a pharmacist telling me my fertility medication was three times the normal amount, tears filled my eyes and I gave up the exhausting journey of trying to conceive. I left it in the hands of Jesus that day. Just four weeks later, I found out we had conceived on our own. It was a beautiful display of a story of God's light in darkness. My message to anyone facing a wall today is to submit your plans to God. Let Him know that you are surrendering it all to His plan, and not your own. I promise, it won't be dark forever, no matter the circumstances. God's light will shine, and as we submit to His will and embrace His plans, His glory will be revealed in our lives (even if it doesn't look like we think it should).

Prayer

Father, I release my will, my wants, and my desires into Your care. I embrace Your perfect will for my life. You know my desires, Lord. You know what I want, and I surrender it all to You. In Jesus' name. Amen.

Hope in His Word

And this hope will not lead to disappointment.
For we know how dearly God loves us,
because He has given us the Holy Spirit to
fill our hearts with His love.

ROMANS 5:5

Feeling in control of your life reduces the amount of vulnerability you feel. It's when you don't know what's going on, what's next, or how things will turn out that the uncomfortable feeling of being vulnerable rises. Being vulnerable is described as being open to attack, harm, or damage.

What God wants to share with us is that in the confines of His will, and even when we get it wrong, we are never vulnerable because of His love for us. This isn't to say things will always go our way or the pains of life will never come. It's to say that we are safe no matter what happens and God is faithful in our lives. We can rest assured when we put our hope in the One who knows all that even when things don't feel good, they are for our good.

Why not speak this truth out loud over yourself, over your children, and over your family members today? You can use your voice to declare what the Word of God says about you and your family when you feel the most vulnerable. Our Creator has given us the authority to cast down negative thoughts that exalt themselves against the Word of God. This hope in His Word will not lead us to disappointment. It will give us renewed strength. It will cause us to collide with the love of Jesus Christ.

Prayer

Father, I know that every day is not going to feel great,
but help me to see You in the midst of feeling vulnerable.
I know You are here with me, with us. I embrace Your love,
Your truth, and Your way. In Jesus' name. Amen.

Gratitude over Worry

Don't worry about anything; instead, pray about everything.
Tell God what you need, and thank Him for all He has done.

PHILIPPIANS 4:6

Mark this page. Whenever you are in a place of having more needs than the resources to provide for them, come to this page and remember this divine direction. All throughout Scripture God gives us formulas on how to live and walk by faith. Today's Scripture verse is one I have next to my desk. Worry is something that comes easily if we aren't careful and if we aren't speaking God's Word over our lives and the lives of our family members. Worry can become like a cancer to our faith. It will erode the spiritual insight and vision of how to take the next step.

I imagine that while you are on this journey, you are experiencing some days when you worry. There is no condemnation for that, just encouragement to refocus. Refocus your eyes on the One who owns all things and knows your journey before you do. This Scripture advises us to get specific. Write down exactly what you are believing God for and then thank Him for all He has done. Having a thankful and grateful heart repositions our minds away from what God hasn't done to what He is or already has done. We can all list a few things that we are grateful to God for. This two-part exercise will position you to reduce the worry and embrace faith.

Think of worry as a crossroads. With one path, you have the option to choose worry, speaking it out loud or allowing others to speak their worry onto you. Or with the other path, you can declare God's truth. You can stand on faith, being a living testimony to those around you who are frozen in fear.

Prayer

Father, I release all worrying thoughts to You.
I release every worrying word that doesn't line up
with Your will for my life. I embrace faith.
Here is what I need from You. (List your needs to God.)
Thank You for all You have done for me.
I'm forever grateful for Your love.
In Jesus' name. Amen.

Building Faith Muscles

Consider it pure joy, my brothers and sisters,
whenever you face trials of many kinds, because you know
that the testing of your faith produces perseverance.
Let perseverance finish its work so that you may be
mature and complete, not lacking anything.

JAMES 1:2–4 NIV

Truth is, troubles will come our way. But we have an advantage because of our faith in Jesus. We have the Word of God that we put our trust in. And when our faith is tested, that is when we shine the brightest. We become walking Bibles as we trust in Him. Some people may never go to church, but they may hear your story. This is why we should view the troubles in our lives with great joy. Through the testing of our faith, our endurance begins to grow. One thing you can hold on to is that your endurance has a place of being fully developed, perfect and complete.

The beautiful thing is that the Word of God reveals you will get to a place of needing nothing. That place is real. It's powerful, it's reassuring, and it's made up of faith. Everywhere you go, you see God, you see faith, you see God's love. Even in the darkest places, you find yourself wanting to be a light, a hope, and a means of reconciliation. When we get to the place of needing nothing, the world no longer has a grip on our desires. We can scroll through social media admiring without desiring. We can communicate with anyone without the need to be right or get the last word.

We can be in a position to give rather than get in our relationships too. It's a beautiful process found through endurance. Endurance is usually connected to the idea of sports because athletes are often pushed to their physical limits, but just imagine allowing the weight of faith to strengthen your endurance over time so you build your faith muscles. Let God build them. Don't run from it. Don't try to change it. Surrender to it. You are being renewed and reformed into the image Christ had when He created you.

Prayer

Father, I trust You in the midst of any trouble I'm currently in or that's coming my way. I surrender to this plan, and I seek Your peace and Your joy. Help me endure the testing of my faith. I release the desire to figure it out or to escape. I give this issue, concern, or problem to You God. I give my life to You. In Jesus' name. Amen.

CHRIST MAY

DWELL IN

YOUR HEARTS

THROUGH FAITH—

THAT YOU,

BEING ROOTED

AND GROUNDED

IN LOVE.

Ephesians 3:17 ESV

Wisdom Through It All

If you need wisdom, ask our generous God, and He will give
it to you. He will not rebuke you for asking. But when you ask
Him, be sure that your faith is in God alone. Do not waver,
for a person with divided loyalty is as unsettled as a wave of
the sea that is blown and tossed by the wind. Such people
should not expect to receive anything from the Lord.
Their loyalty is divided between God and the world,
and they are unstable in everything they do.

JAMES 1:5–8

Divided loyalty. What makes a person have divided loyalty? Walking by faith is largely, if not 100 percent, walking in the unseen world. It goes against everything that comes naturally to us. Walking in God's Spirit takes practice. Let's admit that it's not easy to walk into something when we have no idea how it will end. We put our faith, hope, and trust in God. As God reveals Himself in the midst of the unseen and our faith starts to show itself in physical ways, we grow in our confidence.

The beginning of my faith journey was anything but comfortable as I stepped out to do what I believed God was asking of me. Years later, I still get uncomfortable when I sense God leading me in an unknown direction. Yet God advises us to ask for wisdom. Wisdom has three meanings as described in Merriam-Webster: "Knowledge that is gained by having many experiences in life; the natural ability to understand things that most other people cannot understand; and knowledge of what is proper or reasonable."

Walking by faith through our experiences will give us wisdom. We gain wisdom and understanding through the journey. Our ability to understand things that most other people cannot occurs when the God gives us wisdom about a situation.

This promise of wisdom, found in today's Scripture, is one that God says He will give to us willingly. Our part is to have faith in God alone. Our loyalty cannot be divided between seeking the world's wisdom and seeking godly wisdom. Ask yourself if your loyalty to God is divided. If so, make it your mission to give all your loyalty to God and then ask for wisdom in your relationships, marriage, parenting, career, health, business, ministry, volunteer endeavors, finances, and so on. When He gives you direction, trust Him even if you don't understand the way.

Prayer

Father, I release my loyalty to this world.
God, I ask for wisdom in all areas of my life.
Help me to see You as I walk this faith journey.
God, I want to be guided by You. Make my life
a living testimony for Your glory! In Jesus' name. Amen.

Complete Victory

No, despite all these things,
overwhelming victory is ours through Christ,
who loved us.

ROMANS 8:37

Don't you just love watching the Olympics every four years? Not only do we get to watch competitions in sports we rarely see, like synchronized swimming, we also get to see athletes who have trained for years perform in a matter of minutes and sometimes seconds. Their training comes down to this one moment that could transform their lives.

Track events are one of my favorites to watch. One year, during the 400-meter race, it looked like everyone was running together in the beginning. Then about halfway through the race a runner began to emerge to take the lead. When the pack started together, this particular runner stayed near the back, but then she shifted into high gear during the last leg. She ran so fast with her long legs making strides like a cheetah in a sprint. Her distance from the pack was large—there was no question that she was the winner.

God wants us to know that no matter what happens in life, no matter if we are in the back of the pack and it seems like we are behind, He has given us overwhelming victory! That means in the

end there will be no doubt about who will win this race! It will be THROUGH Christ and His love for us that the world will witness the glory of God shift us into high gear as He leads us to the finish line. We must hold tight to this truth, especially when we feel like we aren't winning in life. The next time you're faced with difficult circumstances and negative thoughts begin to consume you, start with NO. Then finish by reading out loud today's verse from Scripture.

Prayer

Father, thank You for complete victory even when I don't see it. I release all negative talk about my situation or my family's situation. I will speak Your Word, Your will, and Your promises over my situation. In Jesus' name. Amen.

Rest in God's Power

My soul, wait in silence for God alone,
For my hope is from Him.

PSALM 62:5 NASB

One of the greatest lessons I've learned over the years is that God can do more in my resting than in my doing. My relationship with Him is grounded in obedience rather than performance. It sometimes seems as if I need to do something to show God I'm doing my part. While many times we do have a part, there are also times when the instructions are simply to rest. This part of your journey will stretch you just as much as the others, especially for those who are workers by nature.

I am one who is self-motivated, and I don't need much direction to get going. When I came home from working full-time and my first assignment from God was to do the dishes, I knew something must be weirdly off. I couldn't imagine that doing small chores around the house would be in the will of God. Moment by moment and day by day God began to show me His faithfulness in the midst of the dishes, laundry, and meal planning. He began to not only provide for our family but give me purpose in it all as well.

As a stay-at-home mom it's easy to feel like you have lost yourself in the midst of it all. I encourage any mom who is at home with her children that your job is powerful and purposeful. Yes, the dishes need to be done, and yes, the laundry needs to be folded, but as you're folding those clothes, pray for protection for your children. Pray for health for their bodies as you're washing those dishes. That is the power God has given you, and that should never be taken lightly. As we wait on God for our next direction, let us put our hope in Him and focus on the assignment in front of us.

Prayer

Father, thank You for being so very patient with me. I release the need to do it all. I release the desire to be outside of Your will, where I want to please my will and goals. I embrace this season I am in and everything You have called me to do in this hour. I will do it with my whole heart. In Jesus' name. Amen.

Finding Rest

He is so rich in kindness and grace that He purchased our
freedom with the blood of His Son and forgave our sins.
He has showered His kindness on us, along with all wisdom
and understanding. God has now revealed to us His
mysterious will regarding Christ—which is to fulfill His own
good plan. And this is the plan: At the right time He will bring
everything together under the authority of Christ—
everything in heaven and on earth.

EPHESIANS 1:7–10

Don't you just love going on vacation? What is your favorite place to go? The beach? The mountains? A cabin in the woods? One of my favorite places to go is a really nice tropical environment. It took me a while, however, to allow myself the opportunity to rest while on vacation. With so much going on that needed to be done and as a young mom with young children, I found myself struggling as I left everything behind. Once, upon getting to our hotel room, I walked straight to the balcony. It was the view that captivated me. As I sat on the balcony hammock, I didn't have any thoughts to weigh me down. In that moment, looking at what seemed to be an eternity of water with the sun gazing down on the depth of the blue ocean, I finally found rest.

Sometimes my mind jumps quickly from one topic to another. My husband says I must have computer tabs open in my mind. Being on that balcony was everything I didn't know I needed. The quietness allowed the open tabs in my mind to close. It gave me a moment to feel the warm wind as I closed my eyes and listened to the waves of the ocean. I whispered, "God, thank You for this moment." That moment filled me up, and I didn't have to do anything to get the filling. All I had to do was show up.

God wants to give us that vacation-type rest daily in His presence. There's a sweet spot in prayer that offers rest as we close our eyes and close the many tabs of thoughts running around in our minds. It's in that sweet spot that the God's Spirit will breathe on us, allowing us a chance to let it all go. Every worry, every burden, every concern. He wants us to embrace His rest. True rest is found in the presence of God. If we can make it our mission to get that rest daily—and if possible, every now and again on a vacation—then we can see God reveal Himself in a new way as we do less and He does more.

Prayer

Father, thank You for the gift of rest. I release all my mental thoughts and open tabs to You. I ask that You show me how to find my sweet spot and give me the wisdom to come to You there daily. Help me to do less, embracing You as You do more, even when I don't see it. In Jesus' name. Amen.

Peaceful Obedience

*Keep putting into practice all you learned and received
from me—everything you heard from me and saw me doing.
Then the God of peace will be with you.*

PHILIPPIANS 4:9

One of the things I learned from my toddlers is they will mimic everything you do. When I had my firstborn, I was completely taken aback when she started to show me myself. I knew marriage was a mirror, but children are an even bigger mirror making you see yourself in new ways. I'd like to focus on the good things, but I can't help but admit the bad things she did as she was mimicking me. At times I would raise my voice, and she would raise her voice. I would say, "No yelling," and she would say it back to me.

Once my son came along, he showed me my double standards even more. While I was telling him not to do something, he said, "But Mommy, you did it too." Taken aback by his statement, I was at a loss for words because he was right. These were not "do as I say and not as I do" lessons. Those can be quite confusing to children as they are coming into the realization of what's right and what's wrong. If something was wrong, I had to adjust my own actions.

God is asking us to follow His lead. He often gives us direction and shows us how to do something even when we don't understand.

Our job is to listen, receive what He says, and obey Him no matter what the circumstances look like. While Jesus was here, God gave us a living example of what it is to be humble, to pray, to have community, and to lead. The promise behind being obedient is God's peace. God promises us that when we put into action all that we have learned, heard, and seen, peace will be with us. How often do we pray for God's peace without evaluating our own obedience to what He has said?

Prayer

Father, give me clarity and direction that I may obey and do what You have called me to do. I release any stubbornness on my part to follow Your ways. I embrace Your peace today. In Jesus' name. Amen.

Focusing on Things Above

Look, I am the Lord, the God over every creature.
Is anything too difficult for me?

JEREMIAH 32:27 CSB

My husband and I decided to go parasailing during vacation. It looked fun as we watched others from our hotel window. The day for our turn was beautiful. Our instructor shared things we should and should not do while on the ride. As we started to ascend in the air, I got really nervous. The higher I went, the more nervous I became. The sail took us higher and higher. As the wind blew, the sail we were attached to began to sway—and that's when we gave the signal to come down.

I noticed that when I looked down to see how high we were, my anxiety skyrocketed, but when I looked forward to enjoy the view and experience, I felt peace. How often do we find ourselves in situations where we focus on how vulnerable we are, how big the obstacle is, or how far we have to go instead of focusing on how big our God is? When we make it our choice to focus on things above and not on this earth, embracing rest, then we can experience the peace of God that surpasses all understanding.

While the sail we were attached to was swaying high in the sky, there was no reason for me to be calm, except for the fact that I knew who my God was and I felt safe in His care. God is reminding us that nothing is too hard for Him. We must rest in God's promise in today's Scripture verse. Bring your concerns, your cares, your worries, your excitement, and your joys to God. Let this sink in—God can even handle your disappointments and your anger. He longs to talk to you about the things you try to deal with on your own. Today, remember to rest it all at His feet, for God cares for you.

Prayer

Father, thank You for reminding me that nothing is too hard for You. I release any desires or thoughts that cause me to handle the situations of life on my own. Help me to always give them to You as I seek direction and understanding. In Jesus' name. Amen.

God-Given Victory

I have told you all this so that you may have peace in Me.
Here on earth you will have many trials and sorrows.
But take heart, because I have overcome the world.

JOHN 16:33

The summer after graduating from high school was a fun one. I was preparing to enter college and eager to go. I knew that I did not have the finances to go, but I trusted that God would provide. My family was a middle-class working family, but college was very expensive. A few weeks before leaving for school, the funds still had not come in and I found myself very worried, wondering how I was going to pay for school or if I was even going to go. I began to talk to my family, and we decided to pray. I prayed that God would provide and help me have the peace while He worked it out. Five days before I left for college, the provision came in and I was allowed to start school on time. God knew before I did that it would all work out and I would have the victory in that situation.

The word overcome is defined "to conquer." Each day, we have the opportunity to stand on the victory and the overcoming power of Jesus Christ. We are promised through today's Scripture verse that when—not if, but when—the trials and sorrows come, Jesus Christ has already given you the victory over them. This is a great Scripture to stand on as we go through hard times, reminding ourselves that no matter what happens, God has given us the victory. Standing firm on the promises of God is essential in this season of embracing rest. The greatest things you can gain from rest are learning to grow in your faith and realizing God is handling what you can't. God is moving even when we can't see Him. Our needs will be met and God will supply.

Are you finding it hard to silence the noise? Try memorizing Scripture (like today's verse) and reciting it out loud when you need God's peace. Or, spend some time with people will help you find peace in your day. Remember: God can do more with our obedience than He can with our worry.

Prayer

Father, when trials and sorrow come my way, I ask that You release great peace over me. Help me be reminded that I don't have to worry but only need to pray. In Jesus' name. Amen.

A Posture of Humility

So humble yourselves under the mighty power of God,
and at the right time He will lift you up in honor. Give all your
worries and cares to God, for He cares about you.

I PETER 5:6–7

Humility is not a person being silent, unseen, or passive. Humility is when we allow God to take complete control of our lives as we are radically obedient to whatever it is He says. Humility and obedience go hand in hand. Humility is a posture of our hearts as we recognize that God's timing may not be our timing. It is the surrendering of our plans and desires to align with His plans and desires. It is the hope to grow in our love for God's people instead of growing in our position over people. When we recognize that we are all sons and daughters of God, not vying for position or His approval, then thoughts and feelings of being overlooked, unchosen, or abandoned dissipate. What a release it is when we realize that it is not man who promotes us but God and God alone! Godly validation will happen with or without others' approval.

It is so important to have a personal relationship with Jesus Christ—one in which you know when He is leading you in a certain direction or giving you a meaningful message. The wisdom of God will give us clarity in how to follow Him, as it did when the people of

God followed the pillar of cloud by day and the pillar of fire by night as described in Exodus. If God moves us, we must obey. And we must know HOW to obey—whether He says stand still or it's time to move. It's in the HOW that we show our humility. It's in the HOW that we minister to others. It's in the HOW that we love our neighbors. It's in the HOW that we have godly marriages and parent godly children. That HOW is our humility, and it flows out of a heart of prayer and submission to Christ. Spending time in the presence of God gives us a posture of humility, and in His timing, He will exalt the humble.

Prayer

Father, show me my ways. Help me see the areas where I am not humble. Help me to focus not on the next but on the now. Help me be radically obedient in all that You have called me to do. I give my cares to You, God. In Jesus' name. Amen.

Peace of Mind and Heart

I am leaving you with a gift—peace of mind and heart.
And the peace I give is a gift the world cannot give.
So don't be troubled or afraid.

JOHN 14:27

J esus gives amazing gifts such as peace of mind and heart. And how can we tap into these gifts? Sometimes it just a matter of allowing ourselves to rest. With rest, we can get into the habit of letting go of our worries and concerns, and we can exchange them for God's peace of mind.

For many years, I dealt with anxiety. I found myself struggling and having days where I couldn't quite understand what was going on inside. Through counseling I learned that I was experiencing anxiety and at times even panic attacks. This helped me because then I knew what to pray against and what to ask God for deliverance from. My anxiety was rooting in my heart and my emotions. The gifts God placed within me were under attack, and I was able to use God's Word more effectively when I had a better understanding of what was happening to me. After I asked God for deliverance from anxiety, I asked Him for peace of mind and heart.

If you're dealing with something particular, I encourage you to reach out for help and talk to a professional who can help you identify and understand your circumstances so that you can use God's Word more effectively. As for me, I no longer say, "I have anxiety." I changed it to "I am healed of anxiety." In my circumstances, I found that only Jesus and His presence and His Word can get my mind and my heart back to a healthy place. It is so worth it to let Him have the last word over your situation.

Prayer

Father, I give You my mind and my heart. The issues of my heart, the things that plague my mind, I give them over to You. I release all anxiety and panic, as well as any issue that arises within me. Thank You for reminding me that You are the answer. In Jesus' name. Amen.

Remaining in Him

If you remain in Me and My words remain in you,
ask whatever you wish, and it will be done for you.
This is to My Father's glory, that you bear much fruit,
showing yourselves to be My disciples.

JOHN 15:7–8 NIV

You become who you hang around with. Those you hang around become the soil in which the seed you are growing from develops. The beautiful thing about God is that He has given us a way to immediately change our environment. When we get into the presence of God each day, it doesn't matter what our surroundings say about us. His presence creates a new place, new soil. Eventually, He will move us into a better physical environment as we trust in Him.

When you remain in Him, that means you abide in Him, continue in Him. Prayer doesn't have to have a start and stop time as some think. Prayer can be a continuous conversation starting at the beginning of our day. When our thoughts are on Christ, we are remaining in Him. Even as we go to work and complete our task for the day, we remain by allowing Him into every moment. We acknowledge Him in all our ways.

Jesus longs to have a meaningful relationship with you, He wants you to confide in Him no matter what the situation is, no matter where you are. If an issue comes up, ask Him to take care of it. Trusting that God will handle it will produce much fruit. God, our Father, longs to be in our lives in not just big ways but in small, simple, everyday ways as well.

Prayer

Father, from this day forth, help me acknowledge You before I think about anything else. Help me seek You and trust You above all else. In Jesus' name. Amen.

FOR HE WILL

ORDER HIS ANGELS

TO PROTECT YOU

WHEREVER YOU GO.

Psalm 91:11

Fatherly Love

So you have not received a spirit that makes you fearful slaves.
Instead, you received God's Spirit when He adopted you
as His own children. Now we call Him, "Abba, Father."
For His Spirit joins with our spirit to affirm that we are
God's children.

ROMANS 8:15–16

Embracing God as your Father allows you to have peace and rest that doesn't come from any other Source. Some of us have had the unfortunate journey of not having an earthly father or of having an earthly father who was not present in our lives. What that may result in is us struggling to see God as provider, protector, and purifier of our homes and our lives. When our earthly father doesn't give us a godly example from an early age, many of us grow up with vulnerability and an open door for fear, anxiety, and unhealthy connections. These unhealthy connections plant the seeds of fear toward ever having healthy and meaningful relationships.

The lack of a godly father may manifest fear in ways that result in feeling like something bad is about to happen or that things aren't going to work out for our good because "the other shoe is about to drop," as they say. It can also lead to high levels of anxiety if you don't sense that the people you love will stay around you for long. In

addition, fear causes people to feel unlovable. For whatever reason, the seed the absent father plants in a child is a seed of neglect and abandonment and feeling unlovable.

God wants to remind us that He can heal every broken area. He wants to reestablish what it means to be our Father. If you have had a similar experience where you did not have your earthly father in your life like you needed him to be or he was just completely absent and you've never known your dad, God can heal you. He can replace unhealthy seeds that were planted in your heart and show up in your life in ways that make you feel loved, supported, and cared for.

Prayer

Father, thank You for being Abba, Father.
I release all fear that may come from any unhealthy
connections with my parents. I ask that You heal me
today and fill in any gaps that may be present.
In Jesus' name. Amen.

God of the Universe

Oh, how great are God's riches and wisdom and knowledge!
How impossible it is for us to understand His decisions
and His ways!

ROMANS 11:33

One of my favorite places to go with my kids is to the museum. In my city we have a science museum that we all love. There's an area of the museum that shows how tornadoes are formed and how earthquakes occur. I am also fascinated by the solar system and stars exhibit. Everything there goes into great detail about what scientists have discovered. I enjoy learning about the complexities of our universe and how the earth sits in a perfect position in relation to the moon and the sun. As the moon orbits the earth and the earth orbits the sun, together they give the perfect balance for earth to exist as a livable and enjoyable place in the solar system.

This whole system is so very delicate. It reminds me of the human body, which is also featured at the science museum, leaving me in just as much awe. The realization that our body can reproduce life, conceive thoughts, breathe, heal itself, and function as a well-oiled machine is just incredible. Looking at the brain alone will leave your mind blown at how God created us to live and transform in ways that only He could imagine. God's Word tells us His ways and thoughts are higher than our ways and thoughts (Isaiah 55:8–9). We can rest in that truth and trust God, even when we look around and do not fully understand what He is doing.

We must know that He is the God of the universe. The God who is upholding the earth in space and the God of human life and the human brain. He is the God of the weather system, and He can command the wind and rain to be still. He is the God who is able to create and sustain all of this. If He can do all these things, what more can He do in our lives? We can learn to rest in how great our God is. We can also rest in how great His ways are.

Prayer

Father, Your ways are so much higher than my own.
I release my ways to embrace Yours. I release my thoughts
to embrace Yours. Give me greater knowledge of who You are.
In Jesus' name. Amen.

Application is Key

But be doers of the word,
and not hearers only,
deceiving yourselves.

JAMES 1:22 ESV

I have always loved to read and learn. As a child, my mom would take me to the library, and I would get lost in the hundreds of books available for kids or preteens. It excites me to learn about new topics. This hunger has followed me all throughout my life, but one thing I've had to learn to do is to put the books down eventually. I need to actually put into practice what I have learned. Whether that's on topics of marriage, finance, or fitness, the words in the books only give me the tools I need. It is my doing that allows me to apply what I have learned.

We become a force to reckon with when we do more than just read the Bible—when we allow the Bible to transform us and then we act on what we've learned. It's so easy to get caught up in thinking that being a Christian involves following a routine or checking off items in a to-do list. However, the truth is our goal should not be to satisfy our conscience that we did the "Christian thing." Think about it—what would happen if we all decided to apply the messages we hear at church on Sundays instead of just letting the words inspire us momentarily. What would happen if we never put a cap on how we experience God, but rather continue living for Him during every minute of every day? Maybe it's time to ask God to help you carry His love with you through every week of your life.

Prayer

Father, help me to be a doer of Your Word and not only a hearer. I release all distractions or traditions that only allow me to experience You on a one-dimensional level. Flood my life with Your wisdom, Your Word, and worship of You. In Jesus' name. Amen.

Forever Loved

*And I am convinced that nothing can ever separate us
from God's love. Neither death nor life, neither angels
nor demons, neither our fears for today nor our worries
about tomorrow—not even the powers of hell can separate us
from God's love. No power in the sky above or in the earth
below—indeed, nothing in all creation will ever be able to
separate us from the love of God that is revealed in
Christ Jesus our Lord.*

ROMANS 8:38–39

Did you know that one of the strongest things to ever exist in all eternity is God's love for us? Today's Scripture passage says that no power in the sky or in the earth below can separate us from God's love. It goes on to say that nothing in all creation can separate us from God's love. The writer mentions that not even death or life or our fears and worries about tomorrow can separate us from the love of Christ.

It's interesting to me that our fears about today and worries about tomorrow are among the things listed that have the power to separate us from God's love. Our worries and concerns have power. God knows that our fears and worries have so much power in our lives that we need to be reminded that they can't stop His love for us. We tend to respect everything else in these verses, but sometimes we water down this part about our fears and worries. Maybe it's because all of us have worried and feared at some point.

God wants us to know that fear and worry not only destabilize us but are also like a cancer at the very foundation of our faith. He also wants us to know that, if we would allow it, His love can rescue us from a failing foundation. Decide to embrace God's love over your fears. Repeat His Word until you believe it and see it. Know that if God loves you this much, He must have a perfect plan for your life.

Prayer

Father, thank You for Your love. The pursuit of Your love is welcoming and needed. I release the need to understand why You love me. I release my doubt about Your love. I simply embrace all of Your love. Walk with me, God. I need You. In Jesus' name. Amen.

An Amazing Inheritance

The faithful love of the Lord never ends! His mercies never cease. Great is His faithfulness; His mercies begin afresh each morning. I say to myself, "The Lord is my inheritance; therefore, I will hope in Him!"

LAMENTATIONS 3:22–24

When most people think of an inheritance, they think of monetary compensation or acquisition of wealth. Most don't view the Lord as an inheritance. In all actuality, it is our hope and faith in Him that unlocks the keys to the kingdom. When God asks us to seek Him, He is asking us to seek the knowledge of who He is. This knowledge takes us to the place of prayer as our most coveted asset. Prayer is the place where we receive our inheritance. This inheritance is not monetary compensation but an increase in our faith. As our faith increases, our lives increase. There is power in what we believe and what we hope for, and we must recognize that the kingdom currency is faith.

Our inheritance is the Lord because He holds all things together. It is in Him that we learn our plans for the future. It is in Him that we seek everything our hearts desire, and it is also in Him that we find healing for any brokenness we've experienced. Our whole life can be found in Him! The Lord is the greatest inheritance we can ever receive. He consumes us with His mercy and grace and is consistently faithful—there is nothing more we need. Jesus is our greatest inheritance. I am humbled every day by His love. He loved us so much that He died on the cross so that everyone can have the gift of eternal life.

Prayer

Father, thank You for being my inheritance. I embrace You as the greatest resource of my life. I release the trained thought to think that money, things, or even people are the greatest inheritance. It is You, Father. I seek You and the knowledge of who You are. In Jesus' name. Amen.

Submitting to God's Will

The Lord is good to those who wait for Him,
to the person who seeks Him. It is good to wait quietly
for salvation from the Lord. It is good for a man to bear
the yoke while he is still young.

LAMENTATIONS 3:25–27 CSB

One of my first lessons as a believer was learning to depend on God instead of my own actions. It was as if I had to unlearn everything I was taught from an early age. I had been taught to figure out what I wanted and then work hard to get it. So I had to unlearn that hard work pays off for me. Truth is, prayer pays off. My works are only productive through the avenue of faith.

Some find productivity in hard work. If you study hard enough, work enough hours, network enough, or save enough, you can find a level of success. But at what cost? The cost is usually stress, lack of peace, and disappointment that our actions did not reap the results we were pushing for. No one can guarantee that when you put in a certain amount of effort—your time, energy, and sacrifice—you will reap the desired results.

In Christ, however, we can be sure that we will reap not what we want but what He has for us. When we put our trust in Him and release the need to be in control, we give control to the One who holds all control in the first place.

How are we helping our children, and our youth, seek God so they will know how to wait on God as adults. Waiting on Him doesn't always feel good, but it is always good. Waiting on God is an exercise of faith that builds our spiritual muscles. Maybe it's time to ask God how you can help the youth in your community learn this valuable lesson. You never know what He has in store for your gifts and how they can best be utilized. Is it time to share your testimony by volunteering to be a speaker for your youth group? Whatever your gifts are, ask God and be open to hearing from Him the best way you can make an impact on the younger generation.

Prayer

Father, teach me how to wait on You. I release every lesson I learned that is preventing me from embracing Your disciplines. Thank You for Your patience with me. Help me make an impact on the younger generation so they can release it all to You too. In Jesus' name. Amen.

My Refuge and Shield

You are my refuge and my shield;
Your word is my source of hope.

PSALM 119:114

Refuge is defined as the condition of being safe or sheltered from pursuit, danger, or trouble. A shield is defined as a person or thing that provides protection. When I say, "God is my refuge and my shield," it's a declaration that I know God is providing safety for me. How do I know? I know because He has delivered me so many times before and because knowing His Word has made an incredible impact in my life. I know that God is never going to fail me because I've seen His work in action.

Faith is the very substance, the thread, the fabric of things we hope for. "It is the evidence of things we cannot see" (Hebrews 11:1). For example, we can't see the wind, but we know it's there. We feel it on our skin. The evidence of wind is found in the trees swaying or an object moving. The wind identifies itself through the movement of clouds and through our sense of touch as we feel it consume us in the outdoors. Wind can also be created through a fan. The more we feel it, the more we are convinced that it's there. We prepare for it and respond to it with recognition: "Oh, that's wind."

The same goes for God's Word. We must come to recognize its effect all around us and come into the understanding of God's invisible presence, just as we do with the wind. The familiarity with wind makes us prepare for it. How much more should we prepare for God and His Word? We place our hope in His Word because it sustains all living things. That is a refuge and shield we can all rely on.

Prayer

Father, thank You for protecting me. Help me remember that I am safe and always in Your care under Your shield. I release the thoughts that try to convince me that I am unsafe or uncovered. Your Word says I am protected, and I put my trust and hope in that truth. In Jesus' name. Amen.

Power in Weakness

*Yet what we suffer now is nothing compared
to the glory He will reveal to us later. For all creation is
waiting eagerly for that future day when God
will reveal who His children really are.*

ROMANS 8:18–19

My life hasn't been a cakewalk by any means. I've endured a broken family, suicidal thoughts as a thirteen-year-old, bullying in school, being a broke college student on the brink of homelessness, and relationship abuse as a teenager and young adult. Because of all this, I cringe at the idea of suffering. But God revealed to me that His yoke is easy and His burden is light (Matthew 11:30).

I'll never forget the day God let me know the worst was over. Twelve years later He has kept His promise. Still, God wants us to know that no matter what we've been through, there's a glory that will make us all say it was worth the journey. Embracing suffering is not an easy position. It is not for the weak, but His power works best in our weakness (II Corinthians 12:9).

During seasons of suffering my effort or energy usually runs out, and I have no choice but to trust in God. When His faithfulness comes through in my lowest moments, my faith muscle is strengthened. God's Word says without faith it is impossible to please Him. That means seasons of trusting Him are required to embrace this stretching of our faith and the opportunity to grow. Faith produces results; therefore, it pleases God to produce results for us. While it is easier to speak about suffering than to endure it, we know that suffering is necessary and spiritually productive.

Prayer

Father, help me see You in the midst of any suffering that I may endure in my life. I release the need to run from trouble. I know that sometimes You allow things to happen to build up my faith. Help me to grow in maturity and rest in You. In Jesus' name. Amen.

Fly by Faith

Cast your burden upon the Lord and He will sustain you;
He will never allow the righteous to be shaken.

PSALM 55:22 NASB

When you make the decision to allow God to release you, it may at times feel like you're falling. I remember going through this and talking to God through my uncomfortable moments. On one day I said to the Lord, "God, it feels like I'm falling." He said to me, "When you learn to fly by faith, you have to get used to the feeling of falling. In all actuality you are flying." I imagined God being the wind by which my faith wings were held up. I imagined Him as a protective Father. At that time, I learned to flap my wings in an unknown environment. The unknown made me look down and get nervous, but over time I found myself never falling to the ground. I somehow stayed afloat even when I thought I was going to drop. I fell into His grace and love and learned how to fly in the air of faith.

The journey stretched me in ways I never imagined, and now I see God in Scripture in ways I didn't before. I think about Abraham leaving all he knew to obey God, and I think I get it. I think about Ruth and her decision to embrace Naomi, which was a faith walk, and in the process, she found Boaz. I think about Esther and the calling on her life to be brave and bold on behalf of her people. She changed the course of history by her obedience. I'm sure that level of faith wasn't comfortable and was even scary at times.

Yet God's plan prevails as we learn to discern His voice. In these times He reveals Himself to us in beautiful ways. Once God reveals something, everything else can make sense. We can see this to be true in Scripture, but God wants to also show us this in our own lives. He wants to show us that the feeling of falling is oftentimes a great indication that we are walking by faith. Use wisdom and follow God. He will never allow you to fall.

Prayer

Father, thank You for never failing me.
Thank You for showing me the way. I release the tension
I feel from the sense of falling. I ask that You strengthen me
today and for the journey ahead. I'm ready to fly by faith.
In Jesus' name. Amen.

Fully Transparent

O Lord, You have examined my heart and know everything
about me. You know when I sit down or stand up.
You know my thoughts even when I'm far away.

PSALM 139:1–2

The week after our wedding, my husband and I moved into our new apartment. So much had happened that week, and I was glad to finally be settled in. Over the course of the next year there were times when my husband asked me how I was feeling or if something was wrong. Truth is, I had gotten used to dealing with my internal issues alone when I was single. Now that I was married, I found myself having to share because my husband wanted to know what my thoughts were. In the beginning that was uncomfortable. It was difficult to open up consistently when things shifted within me. When I now think about that season of my life, it reminds me that when we open up to God, He already knows what's on our hearts. He knows the thoughts we think, and He is greatly involved in our lives in ways we often don't realize. This should bring us peace, because when we sit down to talk with Him in prayer, there is so much He already understands.

God longs to talk with us about what's going on in our hearts and minds. This can be uncomfortable for someone who is not used to the level of care or concern He offers. Like for me, when I first got married, I had to get used to the idea that my husband could tell when my joy shifted or when something was wrong. I encourage you today to be fully transparent with God—even about the things you don't think He knows or the things you are still learning about yourself. Over the next few days, we will go deeper to discover even more about how God is so involved with us, both internally and externally.

Prayer

Father, since You already know all about me, I just want to say thank You for loving the parts of me that aren't the greatest. Thank You for seeing me for who I am and loving me anyway. In Jesus' name. Amen.

MY SOUL,
WAIT IN SILENCE
FOR GOD ALONE,
FOR MY HOPE
IS FROM HIM.

Psalm 62:5 NASB

Filling Every Void

You see me when I travel and when I rest at home.
You know everything I do. You know what I am going to say
even before I say it, Lord. You go before me and follow me.
You place your hand of blessing on my head. Such knowledge
is too wonderful for me, too great for me to understand!

PSALM 139:3–6

God loves you. I am convinced that the human mind is unable to fully conceive just how much God loves His children. There is a longing inside each of us to be loved and known. We are designed to be filled by God's love. I used to enjoy putting together puzzles with my grandmother. These were large, intricate puzzles that took quite a few hours to complete. With these puzzles, some of the pieces looked like they were the missing piece I needed, but when I went to put them in the puzzle, the pieces wouldn't fit. There was a side edge that didn't match the hole or a protruding part that caused the piece not to fit correctly.

This concept can be related to our relationship with God in many ways. How often do we try to fill the voids in our lives with things that end up leaving us just as empty or even more empty? I can't count how many times I've thought that one thing or another would make me feel whole when actually the only things that can fill me up are

Jesus, His Word, and His presence. He is my missing piece. All His sides fill my soul; there aren't any gaps or empty places.

I experienced this the first time in a church service when I was eleven years old. I had never felt the presence of God like I did that day. I stood up and saw the other young people lifting their hands in worship, and my heart opened that day. For the first time ever, I felt like God wasn't just for adults. He was for me too. The presence of God came into my heart like a flood. At the time I was struggling with a lot of things, but I remember feeling God's presence fill every dark and empty hole within me, and I was never the same again. What areas do you need to allow God to fill? What areas have you tried to fill with other things only to be left feeling even more empty?

Prayer

Father, thank You for loving me. Thank You for knowing me so well. Most importantly, thank You for coming into my heart, filling every void and empty space. I release these areas to Your presence. In Jesus' name. Amen.

Miracle-Working Power

Where can I go from Your Spirit?
Where can I flee from Your presence?
If I go up to the heavens, You are there;
if I make my bed in the depths, You are there.

PSALM 139:7–8 NIV

On the day of my MRI I went into the hospital, got into a gown, and came to a room with a very large machine. In the middle of the machine there was an opening where I would lay. I lay down and closed my eyes as they took images of what would be diagnosed as a pituitary tumor underneath my brain. Weeks before, my body indicated something was off and this tumor was the cause of it. My doctors put me on medication to reduce the size of the tumor. All I could think was, How could this happen?

Apparently, the tumor had formed during an extremely stressful period of my life. Remembering this season made me feel sad because I felt like it was preventable. I felt like I didn't have to be going through this. But it was in this moment that God whispered, "I am here." He reminded me that because He was there everything would be just fine. I cried as the realization that everything would work out settled into my heart. Over the next few years, everything did work out.

I had a huge burden placed on me in the form of a tumor;

however, my God is bigger than the tumor I had. He is bigger than any condition or diagnosis. He is bigger than my fears and my doubts. He goes before me, and it is His strength that supports me. I had to put myself in a place where I knew that whatever happened next, God would never abandon me. I found great peace in knowing that He had a plan and no matter how this diagnosis played out, He was working it out for my good. His plans are always bigger than mine.

While it was difficult to conceive when we were ready to expand our family, God gave me two beautiful miracles and never allowed this condition to consume me. If anything, this situation has been used as a testimony of His miracle-working power. And I am thankful every single day. And that must be our heart's posture—that since You know me, since You go before me, You are also in control. In this, we rest, no matter what.

Prayer

Father, thank You for always going before me.
Thank You for guiding me. I release to You the heaviness
of every burden I'm carrying. In Jesus' name. Amen.

You are Never Too Far Gone

If I ride the wings of the morning,
if I dwell by the farthest oceans,
even there Your hand will guide me,
and Your strength will support me.

PSALM 139:9–10

Going to college was an interesting time for me. I wanted to be free and do whatever it is I wanted to do. I was happy to be able to leave my dorm room at 12:00 a.m. and go to a party or a friend's room if I wanted. I was excited to find my way around campus and meet people all on my own terms. I did all of this. I went to parties, met new people, and had all the fun I had ever wanted. Then one day I was riding a bus to the mall with a group of friends. There were so many people on the bus, you'd think feeling lonely would be the furthest thing from my mind. Truth is, as I was riding on that bus, I felt God's presence. It was as if He was nudging me and saying, "I can fill that void in your heart." He also said, "You haven't gone too far for Me to reach you."

I didn't feel my best hearing God say that because I knew I had shame and guilt. I wasn't being the Christian I knew I could be—I wasn't praying, serving Him, or being an example or disciple like I should have been. I was doing my own thing. I thought that lifestyle

would be fulfilling to me. It wasn't. I longed for the presence of God. I longed to come back into a relationship with Him and to spend time with Him, allowing Him to heal me from all the guilt and shame I carried.

The fact that God pursued me really got my attention. Truth is, looking back, He was always there. No matter how far I went, He was there. I encourage you to believe that no matter how far you go, He will be there. His love is ready to consume you, to embrace you, and to transform you. I didn't change overnight, but one day at a time I experienced more healing and deliverance. I slowly began to let go of certain friends and embrace the God who pursued me.

Prayer

Father, thank You for always being there for me no matter how far away from You I go. I release the run, the guilt, and any shame I may be holding on to, and I ask for forgiveness. I repent and I embrace Your forgiveness. In Jesus' name. Amen.

A New Mindset

I could ask the darkness to hide me and the light around me to
become night—but even in darkness I cannot hide from You.
To You the night shines as bright as day. Darkness and light
are the same to You.

PSALM 139:11–12

In the book of Genesis, when Eve decides to eat the fruit and give it to Adam as well, the Bible speaks about God coming into the garden. Since God is everywhere and knows all things, the question of "Where are you?" to Adam always baffles me. God wasn't asking where they were in the physical sense, though. He was asking about where they were in the spiritual sense. Where were they in the freedom God gave them, where were they in the joy God gave them, and where were they in the confidence God gave them?

Shame and guilt are usually brought on by sin and cause us to be separated from God. Then we run from God. God doesn't run from us. Today's Scripture passage says that to God darkness and light are the same; therefore there is no area too dark where the love of God can't penetrate.

Sometimes we are convinced in our lowest moments in life that God couldn't love us. I used to be sure that because I sinned, I needed to go about my life, hoping His judgment wouldn't fall on me. I had consequences to pay for sure, but even then, His love allowed me the opportunity for redeeming power. I realized that through the process of redemption, His love is most evident. The moment I surrendered was the beginning. I never felt judged by God. I never felt like He didn't have my best interest at heart. I simply felt His love, His guidance, and His direction. I found myself wanting to know more about Him. I wanted to grow deeper in my relationship with this God who loved me at my worst. Through getting to know Him and learning about Him, I found myself in a new mindset and life. I looked up and was no longer bound, no longer depressed, no longer worried. I was redeemed! It all started with His love.

Prayer

Father, Your love is what gives us purpose.
To help others experience Your love is what this life
is all about. I release any other desires and motives
that are contrary to Your purpose. It's all about You.
In Jesus' name. Amen.

Praying for Children

*For you formed my inward parts; you knitted me together
in my mother's womb. I praise you, for I am fearfully
and wonderfully made. Wonderful are your works;
my soul knows it very well.*

PSALM 139:13–14 ESV

It was the last day of my pregnancy, and my labor was going to be induced. I was thirty-nine weeks pregnant with my son. This pregnancy with him started quite hard. Around week eight, I began to have weird symptoms every time I ate. After a meal, I experienced extreme exhaustion and fatigue, and I could not move for forty-five minutes. I'd lie wherever I was or sit with my head down at my desk in my office. It happened so much that I became afraid to eat. I removed dairy from my diet, but it still happened. Along with the intense fatigue, I felt horrible and had the worst mental fog. I could literally stare at a wall and not be bothered.

These symptoms only got worse as the weeks went on. During week ten, I lost ten pounds in seven days and finally had enough. I went to church and asked for prayer that day. During the prayer, the pastor mentioned how this was an attack on me while I was pregnant. After she prayed over me, another woman walked up to me and said she was from Chicago, sent to me to pray over my baby. I never mentioned I was pregnant to anyone, other than the pastor, and this woman was nowhere near me while the pastor was praying over me. It was a miracle. We connected, and I found out her sister was a doula who was also assigned to pray over me and walk with me through this pregnancy.

Later that week, I saw a post online about a woman experiencing mental fog, and it was due to eating gluten. A lot of her symptoms sounded like my symptoms, so I made an appointment with a gastroenterologist. They couldn't do any testing because I was pregnant, but they agreed I should stay away from gluten. That was my last day eating gluten, and all my symptoms cleared up.

Months later, I went to the hospital to be induced and birthed a healthy baby boy. The umbilical cord was wrapped around his neck as he was born, but he was just fine. I've wondered why I couldn't eat gluten, why I experienced spiritual and physical warfare during that pregnancy—only God knows. We believe my son has a call on his life. From the very moment I knew I was pregnant, I knew he would be a boy. After he was born, I looked into his eyes and covered his life in prayer. May we all pray over our children, our children to come, our wombs, and our adopted children. We need to become sensitive to who they are, as God intended them to be.

Prayer

Father, thank You for the miracle of children.
I pray over all my children that Your divine will be done
in their lives and that every detail of their lives will be fulfilled
in the way You designed it to be. In Jesus' name. Amen.

God Is Always Near

You watched me as I was being formed in utter seclusion,
as I was woven together in the dark of the womb.
You saw me before I was born. Every day of my life was
recorded in Your book. Every moment was laid out
before a single day had passed.

PSALM 139:15–16

Over the past few days, we have been diving into Psalm 139 and talking about how God is so very involved in our lives. Whenever you're at a place in your life where you feel like you're unsure about what's happening, this is a great psalm to come back to and speak out loud. God is sharing with us here that He is an involved Father. He wants us to know that no matter how our life goes, no matter if we can control our circumstances, all it takes to move in a positive direction is a decision to do things His way.

God understands that life may feel dark at times, but His love prevails. We have to remove the perception that God's love only appears in one form or for certain people. Unfortunately, social media has made it seem like God's love and favor are only for a select few, but the truth is, God's love is expressed in many ways. You don't have to have a million dollars, drive the latest vehicle, have the most elite friends, or be the most popular to experience the love of God. You can experience God's love right where you are.

Let me share something with you about God. He will never barge His way into your life. He is a perfect gentleman. He waits to be invited. The most powerful thing God gave all of us is the ability to choose. The ability to choose in a situation whether it is dark or light. The ability to choose Him when we understand what's going on or when we are totally oblivious to what it is that He is doing. It is in this choice that we also welcome the love that He has for us. Change your perspective. It is not that He's not there; it's that He's waiting to come in.

Prayer

Father, You are welcome here. Come into my whole life.
I release my doing, my way, my plans. I give You complete
control over every area. In Jesus' name. Amen.

Questions for God

How precious are Your thoughts about me,
O God. They cannot be numbered! I can't even count them;
they outnumber the grains of sand! And when I wake up,
You are still with me!

PSALM 139:17–18

I'm a thinker. Thankfully, my husband is a great listener, as he often hears all the thoughts going on in my mind on any given day. I know my many thoughts are a lot for him to handle, but to think, as today's verses say, that our God has more thoughts than the grains of sand about me, now I don't feel so bad.

If God has this many thoughts about us, we can literally ask God anything we want. During this time of rest, make it your mission to ask God as many questions as you can and give Him the space to answer those questions. You might think you are bothering God, but He's thinking of you! He wants to share with you, so you can never bother God.

Make a list of your most pressing questions. Write them out and one by one ask God a question each day. When He answers you, mark that the question is answered. This is a fun way to converse with God daily. Also, there is no limit to how many questions you can ask, and no question is off-limits. He can handle any question from you.

It can be something deep and hard from your past or something light and current like a question about your food.

Prayer

Father, thank You for every thought You have about me. I would love to know more of Your thoughts about me and Your perspective on how You created me and the gifts You have given me. I release myself from any idea that my questions aren't welcome, and I plan to have more conversations with You. In Jesus' name. Amen.

Unshakable Faith

"Daughter," He said to her, "your faith has saved you.
Go in peace and be healed from your affliction."

MARK 5:34 CSB

One of the most powerful stories in the Gospels is about a woman with a bleeding issue. After going to doctors and spending tons of money to be healed of her condition, she actually got worse. I can identify. I can remember a few times when I had issues with my tumor, including the time when the doctors gave me a dose of a medication and I ended up in the emergency room with an allergic reaction. During these times, I became discouraged. Then there were times when I had unshakable faith. I'd look at my condition and know that if only I could touch God with my faith, I would be made whole.

Jesus was in a crowd that day with the bleeding woman, and many people touched Him. What made her touch different from others? It was her faith. She was desperate to get to Jesus and knew her answer was right in front of her face. This shows that the hunger of faith gets God's attention more than most things. It is a decision to reach for Him in spite of what the circumstances reveal. When we reach for God, we pull on Him and He responds. Our plans, A–Z, must be God. Having a "just in case" plan waters down our faith. Having an "only God plan" ignites the space in our lives for God to not only move but also to reveal Himself in whatever capacity that He will.

This is the perfect opportunity for us as believers to be transformed as we walk on a new level of faith knowing God more intimately. I am sure after this woman touched Jesus' garment and He declared that it was her faith that made her whole and healed, that her faith grew to new levels. The other part of this story is the witness she became for others. I can't count how many times God's power and glory has been revealed through my belief in Him. On this journey of transformation, what are you believing God for?

Prayer

Father, thank You for this story. I reach for You, God. I release my plans that do not include You. I release the mindset that tries to separate You from other parts of my life. You are my life. In Jesus' name. Amen.

A Deep Faith

Loving God means keeping His commandments,
and His commandments are not burdensome.
For every child of God defeats this evil world,
and we achieve this victory through our faith.
And who can win this battle against the world?
Only those who believe that Jesus is the Son of God.

I JOHN 5:3–5

In college I became friends with a girl who had a deep faith. As our friendship grew, I realized that she followed God closely and never did anything that He didn't tell her to do. She made plans based on what He laid upon her heart. Her confidence in belief came from a deep place. She got into the habit of trusting God no matter what was going on. Her belief and her deep faith bled into all areas of her life.

I believe God introduced this friend to me for a reason. The more I witnessed her lean into His guidance without any worry or fear or hesitation, the more I wanted what she had. He highlighted her in a way that made me ask, "What is she doing? How is she doing it?" It made me curious about her faith, and it led me to some much-needed self-reflection. I believed, but did I believe without any doubt or concern? This friend inspired me to look at my faith journey and ask some real hard questions. And because I went through that process,

I hope to inspire others as they see me learn and grow strong in my belief. After all, we will be set up on a hill that can't be hidden so the world will know that only God could do that. And hopefully, the world will want to know more about Him. It is always all about Him.

Prayer

Father, show me the areas in my life that are eroding my faith. Show me the areas that I can be strengthened in my faith. I want to follow You in all I do. In Jesus' name. Amen.

A Nurturing Nature

You were cleansed from your sins when you obeyed the truth,
so now you must show sincere love to each other as brothers
and sisters. Love each other deeply with all your heart.

I PETER 1:22

When I first started gardening, I learned a lot of things about life, planting, harvesting, and so on. I learned some plants need a lot of water and a lot of sun while other plants need shade and a little water every now and then. It's true, there's not one plant that has the exact same needs as another.

One day my garden was struggling. The heat outside became intense and even the plants that loved sunlight were in desperately needed some water. The leaves on my hanging plants were down and hanging over. At that moment I spoke to my plants and gave them some love through water and fertilizers. I tended to the garden to make sure it was a comfortable place to live. After I walked in the house to put away my gardening supplies, I came back out to find that the leaves had perked up and the plants weren't leaning over anymore. It happened within a few minutes! By nurturing and caring for them they looked better very quickly. While the water and fertilizer probably did the trick, I have to say there's a part of me that wonders if my loving words didn't play a small role in the revitalization.

All this to say, how much more can we change our families, communities, and the world by the love we show? How deeply do you love those around you? Our greatest act as Christ followers is how we love others.

Prayer

Father, thank You for reminding me of this truth.
Help me be a conduit of Your love for people.
I release all bitterness, unforgiveness, and barriers
that are preventing me from being cleansed and healed.
In Jesus' name. Amen.

SEE, I AM SENDING
AN ANGEL BEFORE YOU
TO PROTECT YOU
ON YOUR JOURNEY
AND LEAD YOU SAFELY
TO THE PLACE I HAVE
PREPARED FOR YOU.

Exodus 23:20

SO HUMBLE YOURSELVES

UNDER THE MIGHTY

POWER OF GOD,

AND AT THE RIGHT TIME

HE WILL LIFT YOU UP IN HONOR.

GIVE ALL YOUR WORRIES

AND CARES TO GOD,

FOR HE CARES ABOUT YOU.

I Peter 5:6–7

Peace in His Presence

I have been crucified with Christ and I no longer live,
but Christ lives in me. The life I now live in the body,
I live by faith in the Son of God, who loved me
and gave Himself for me.

GALATIANS 2:20 NIV

One evening, I was relaxing with my family while watching a documentary about a deep dive into the ocean. The divers got inside a round submarine that was clear so they could see underwater. As they went deeper into the ocean, new rules applied about survival. Due to the pressure around them, they could not just jump out into the water. Our bodies can only handle the pressure of water around us to a certain depth. These divers allowed themselves to be immersed in such a way—the submarine they were in—that the rules literally changed.

When we allow our lives to be immersed in Jesus, dying to our old way of life, we enter God's kingdom, where there are new rules. These new rules allow us to experience a depth of God that is only experienced in the reality of submission to Him. Laying down our old lives is not easy, yet it is necessary so that we may walk in the faith of our Lord Jesus Christ.

When we are in the presence of Jesus, we cannot be persuaded by outside forces. When we are surrounded by God, we have no need to worry, we have no need to strive for more, we have no need to look for approval from others. In fact, when we fully surrender our lives to His love, our focus changes from how we can get ahead to how we can serve others. How can we help others experience the kingdom of God?

Prayer

Father, I release my old self and die to my old life.
I ask that You live in me as I walk in complete, total,
and radical obedience for Your glory.
In the name of Jesus. Amen.

The Ultimate Builder

"For I know the plans I have for you," says the Lord.
"They are plans for good and not for disaster, to give you a
future and a hope. In those days when you pray, I will listen.
If you look for Me wholeheartedly, you will find Me."

JEREMIAH 29:11–13

During the building of our home, I saw the architectural plans maybe once or twice. Since I am not very analytical, I was okay with the plans as long as the house was safe. Through the many months that it took to build the house, I began to see the house take shape out of what was once unfinished land. At first, there was just land and then just a slab of concrete followed by unpainted walls, empty spaces where appliances would go, and slowly but surely it developed into a house—the place we call home today. When I think about this in connection with our lives, I realize we often see our lives as unfinished. We are always waiting to arrive, always striving for the housewarming party, always thinking life will be better once we get the refrigerator in place. But what we don't realize is that sometimes our lives don't look like anything we've prayed for, and things certainly don't happen at the speed we want them to happen. Yet God gives us reassurance that His plans are for good and not for disaster.

In today's Scripture (Jeremiah 29:11–13), God was speaking to His people about what was to come as they were in exile. These words are also a promise to us of how God works. He will never leave us in circumstances that are not for our good. When we put our faith and trust in Him, we can be confident that this current situation doesn't compare to what He is building in our lives. If we could allow the Ultimate Builder to take His plans—with every detail, setback, and unknown circumstance—to create a life that brings glory to His name, we'd see how His plans were good for us all along. It's easy to get tripped up in unknown or unexpected things that happen. But God simply tells us to pray, and He promises He will listen. I've learned that the unknown is an invitation to go deeper and learn more about Him. What unknowns do you have in your life right now? Can you see these situations as invitations to experience God in new ways?

Prayer

Father, thank You for always having perfect plans.
I place my hope in You and release my future into Your care.
In Jesus' name. Amen.

Being Like Jesus

Imitate God, therefore, in everything you do,
because you are His dear children.

EPHESIANS 5:1

Being a mom has been the most beautiful and challenging experience I've ever gone through. I thoroughly enjoy being a mom to my children, but it wasn't until they started to walk, talk, and grow that another element of being a mom came into shape. They started doing what they saw me doing. They began to say the things I'd say and eat what I ate. It was as if I was showing them how to live. This completely took me by surprise because for the first time ever, I had to watch my own actions. I was much more careful with what I did because these little people were copying me.

The pressure was real, and I was faced with the reality that I was not a perfect human being. I needed to teach my children by apologizing and asking for forgiveness when I was wrong. I realized I need to display these traits with everyone I influence. Whose ways should I follow and how should I respond? God's ways are beautiful and give me a greater understanding of His love for His people. I still have a long way to go, but one thing I know is God's way always turns out better for both parties involved. He has a way of requiring humility, patience, long-suffering, wisdom, and more.

Truth is, it's Jesus who helps me imitate God. I want to think like Him, even though my thoughts aren't like His and His ways are so far higher than mine. I want to love like Him and give to the needy as He did when He walked the earth. I want to forgive like He does—going so far as to forgive those who killed and betrayed Him. His is the perfect example, and now my mission is to point my children to more of Him and less of me. May we all find grace, mercy, and direction as we imitate Him.

Prayer

Father, thank You for being the ultimate leader.
You have given us the correct responses to every situation
life can throw at us. I release the need to do things my own
way and embrace how You would do it. In Jesus' name. Amen.

Restored and Renewed

Who pardons all your guilt, Who heals all your diseases;
Who redeems your life from the pit, Who crowns you with
favor and compassion; Who satisfies your years with good
things, So that your youth is renewed like the eagle.

PSALM 103:3–5 NASB

The journey of transformation isn't one that happens overnight. It can often feel like you take three steps forward and then one step back. God understands that we may get things wrong at times. We may not make the right decisions or we may make mistakes while trying to do what is right. That is what His grace and mercy are for. I encourage you to submit your weaknesses to God as you are being transformed daily. Share them with Him so He can show you a lesson in the setback.

I have learned throughout life to embrace failure. Failure has given me a new perspective and has humbled me to be teachable. As we are all transformed, let us have a heart posture of learning. My kids are at an age where they ask tons of questions, and every now and then they will tell me when they think my answer is wrong. It's cute at this age, but when they get older, it is my hope they will be humble and realize just how much we don't know. We all need God—from the smartest, most articulate person in the room to the one struggling to put words together.

God is holding this world together, and for those who will listen, He has amazing things to share. He longs to love us and fill our lives with good things. Our part is simply to come to Him and seek Him with everything in us. When we receive His forgiveness and healing, we are renewed!

Prayer

Father, thank You for Your Word. Thank You for forgiving me of all my sins and healing me of all my diseases. I release my journey of transformation to You. I lay it down at Your feet. Build me into who You want me to be. In Jesus' name. Amen.

Consistent Discipline

No discipline is enjoyable while it is happening—it's painful!
But afterward there will be a peaceful harvest of right living
for those who are trained in this way.

HEBREWS 12:11

Two nights a week my children have a little bit of homework given to them by their teachers. My daughter doesn't mind her homework, except for the times when she longs to play with her toys. It's during these times that I remind her that her hard work will pay off with long-term effects. She eventually gives in and decides to finish her work. After many weeks of this, I received a call from her teacher that would make any parent proud. Her teacher let me know that my daughter had improved in school and that she had done very well on her latest assessment. We had never gotten such an encouraging call; it truly blessed us.

I also had to remember long-term goals when I wanted to lose twenty pounds. In the beginning I had to make such drastic changes to my diet. I had to think about the end goal more than the present discomfort. I thought about how I have complete control over what I put in my body. When I reached for something with my hand and put it to my mouth, what was in my hand was totally up to me. That freedom was beautiful, but if I wasn't careful with what I reached for and put in

my mouth, my health would have deteriorated, and I wouldn't have felt my best—all because of my own choices and decisions.

Discipline is not a word that most people love. It requires a high level of consistency and redundancy that can be a challenge, unless you are naturally inclined to it. God wants to encourage us in this area of discipline. When we live with discipline, we will reap a harvest. But did you know that discipline can be negative? That's right. If you are disciplined in eating the wrong food, going without much water, or getting into unhealthy relationships, that consistency will pay off, just not in your favor. On the contrary, when we make consistent choices that align with where we want to go, that also pays off. What choices and decisions do you need to make today to reap the peaceful harvest of right living?

Prayer

Father, help me see the areas where I am not disciplined.
I release the stubbornness that has convinced me to not become
my best self. Help me to change. In Jesus' name. Amen.

Your Spirit, Not Your Size

They started arguing over which of them would be most famous. When Jesus realized how much this mattered to them, He brought a child to His side. "Whoever accepts this child as if the child were Me, accepts Me," He said. "And whoever accepts Me, accepts the One who sent Me. You become great by accepting, not asserting. Your spirit, not your size, makes the difference."

LUKE 9:46–48 *THE MESSAGE*

Look again at the end of today's Scripture passage. It is worth repeating. "Your spirit, not your size, makes the difference." This statement couldn't be truer than in the current climate with so many people desiring to have more followers, fame, and money. The things we are dealing with in our society are not new to humankind. While technological and economic advances have been made, and while the world has changed culturally, there have always been some fundamental things we desire as human beings.

Today's Scripture highlights that even in the presence of Jesus, people were desiring to be famous. We all have that internal desire to be seen, to be bigger, to have the most influence. Using a child is a great lesson for us all. A child doesn't know much, is usually teachable, asks a lot of questions, makes a lot of mistakes, needs leadership and direction, and so on. Yet God is saying, "The way you accept this child is how you will accept Me and ultimately My Father. When you accept this child with humility and understanding, you accept Me."

A profound part of this passage is the statement "You become great by accepting, not asserting." So what is it about accepting that makes us great? Accepting Jesus by faith is what makes us great. No matter how it may look, no matter how the circumstances turn out, when God shows up, we must accept His plans and His ways—all of Him. Accepting means "giving consent to receive something that is offered or recognizing something as valid and correct." That is how you become great. When you believe and recognize that Jesus is not only valid but correct, you step into a level of greatness that can only be revealed through accepting Him.

Prayer

Father, I know at times it feels like the goal is to be bigger, better, and recognized in order to claim success.
I release this need and embrace Your idea of being great.
In Jesus' name. Amen.

Protecting Peace

*Then you will experience God's peace, which exceeds anything
we can understand. His peace will guard your hearts and
minds as you live in Christ Jesus. And now, dear brothers
and sisters, one final thing. Fix your thoughts on what is true,
and honorable, and right, and pure, and lovely, and
admirable. Think about things that are excellent and worthy
of praise. Keep putting into practice all you learned and
received from me—everything you heard from me and
saw me doing. Then the God of peace will be with you.*

PHILIPPIANS 4:7–9

Peace is like faith. It is one of the most powerful things in God's kingdom. The disruption of our peace can disrupt multiple areas of our lives. It's important to guard our peace by guarding our thoughts. How do we guard our thoughts? We do it by concentrating on the good news. What is the good news? That Jesus died for our sins and has risen with all power in His hands. Since that is the case, nothing can ever come against us when we believe! The good news is that we are all saved by grace through faith. The good news is Jesus lives! That gives us peace that surpasses all understanding and protects our hearts as well as our minds.

We must embrace Jesus and His death on the cross so that our sins are wiped away. Because He has done this for us, we can come into a divine relationship with Him by simply believing that He is! Let us remember this whether we are seasoned Christians or new believers. God has given us peace. When our thoughts start to go every which way, we can remember what He did on the cross and the power He claimed in that one move. Our faith is in Him!

Prayer

Father, thank You for dying on the cross for me.
I ask for Your peace to invade my life, my heart, and my mind.
Give me wisdom on how to protect the gift of peace at all times.
In Jesus' name. Amen.

Character Building

Until the time came to fulfill his dreams,
the Lord tested Joseph's character.

PSALM 105:19

A mentor once told me that revelations will get you in the room, education will keep you in the room, but it is your character that will show you how far you go outside the room. This was powerful to me because I've had to learn that God has not been trying to hold me back or leave me with unanswered prayers. My many years of learning were building my character. I'm so grateful that God doesn't give us what we think we want at the time we think we want it.

As we allow God to grow us, we learn about ourselves in ways we never even imagined. When I pray now, I preface my prayers by saying, "God, please do not give me anything I'm not ready for and that my character can't sustain." Character is built in the valley moments. The places when it feels like we are overlooked, unseen, and complete failures. In these times, we are taught things about ourselves that only valley moments can reveal. These are moments when we pray and God gives us a glimpse of what we're asking for to show us how much we aren't ready for it.

This happened to Joseph. I love the story of Joseph because God gave him a dream, a promise of what was to come, and it took many years of hard times and even betrayal before he was walking in the promises of God. The experiences he suffered through—from being sold by his brothers, to Potiphar's wife lying about him, to time in jail—were all building his character.

Do you remember a time when you felt like life was caving in on you and hardship was coming from all sides? Could it be that God was using this to build your character and reveal gifts that are inside of you? I wonder if Joseph had never experienced the sequence of events that led him to Potiphar if he would have even known that he could interpret dreams so well. We often speak against difficult times, but what good lies in the lessons of character-building? It's not easy. I've been there many times. But seeing who I am now because of the hard times has given me compassion, humility, and ultimately divine favor to fulfill God's will.

Prayer

Father, I know that character-building is not always easy,
but thank You for the times that You loved me enough
to take me through it. I release the fear of character-building,
and I hold tight in faith that You will carry out Your will.
In Jesus' name. Amen.

In Loving Pursuit

Whoever pursues righteousness and kindness will find life, righteousness, and honor.

PROVERBS 21:21 ESV

What is your greatest pursuit at this moment? If you could go back over the last twenty-four hours, what would you say you thought about the most? Better yet, what did you spend your time and resources on? These questions will help guide you into understanding what you are pursuing. If you find it is not God, that you are not pursuing Him with your whole heart and soul, make the necessary changes now. This journey of transformation can happen, but it takes you doing your part.

A few years ago, I went to God in prayer about having a baby. During my times of prayer, I sensed God wanted me to become vegetarian. It was as if He said, "You do your part, and I will do Mine." My part was simply surrendering. And that's true for you too. When we are in fierce pursuit of our goals, our visions, and our plans, surrendering can feel unnerving. We're left asking, why am I doing all of this and is God pleased? Make a change and stand on the promise offered in today's Scripture that when you pursue righteousness and unfailing love, you will find life, righteousness, and honor. These are three gifts God wants to give you in His way and in His time. His timing is perfect no matter how we see things. He knows all things—

what's going on in the world and what our lives can handle. Trust Him before and during your pursuit of Christ through your transformation.

Prayer

Father, thank You for these promises. I release my pursuits to You. No matter how hard it is, I want to give up my own pursuits to pursue more of You. In Jesus' name. Amen.

Tending to Your Garden

Then Christ will make His home in your hearts as you trust in Him. Your roots will grow down into God's love and keep you strong. And may you have the power to understand, as all God's people should, how wide, how long, how high, and how deep His love is. May you experience the love of Christ, though it is too great to understand fully. Then you will be made complete with all the fullness of life and power that comes from God.

EPHESIANS 3:17–19

The garden of our soul is a place that needs constant tending. In my home garden I need to make sure there are no weeds growing, do my best to keep it fertilized and full of nutrients, add soil when needed, and spray the plants so bugs don't get to them. I can have weeds in my spiritual garden too. Through the years I've learned that bitterness and unforgiveness can grow below the surface for so long that by the time they sprout, they have roots that run deep throughout my garden, choking the life out of the next living thing. Bitterness, unforgiveness, anger, pride, and fear are just a few strong weeds that can grow in our soul gardens. We must uproot every weed and unhealthy thought pattern by confessing them and asking God to take us through the process of getting those issues removed from our hearts.

It is the same with what some call the "orphan spirit." This is the feeling that we are overlooked, neglected, unseen, forgotten, and at the root of it, rejection. Feeling abandoned can lead to broken relationships. These feelings can also lead to an overachiever attitude that's based on performance. Many people unknowingly live with these feelings and never take the steps to heal. To move past this in your life, ask yourself if you experience any of the feelings mentioned earlier. Even if you only occasionally face these feelings, why not pray and ask God to heal you, to remind you that you are accepted by Christ, and to fill you with His Fatherly love?

When we realize that we are sons and daughters of God, there is nothing extra that we need to do to be loved. Just being with our Father is enough. His love is not conditional. He will love us anyway we are, and His love can't change. Coming into the understanding of this love is what causes the filter system to our heart to ignite, and over time, Jesus purifies us through our faith in Him.

Prayer

Father, thank You for loving me in so many ways.
I release any resentment, overwhelm, and performance-based
mindset that's within me. I ask that You help me see and know
the way forward. In Jesus' name. Amen.

YOU ARE MY REFUGE

AND MY SHIELD;

YOUR WORD IS MY

SOURCE OF HOPE.

Psalm 119:114

Wonderfully Made

God created human beings in His own image.
In the image of God He created them; male and female
He created them. Then God blessed them and said,
'Be fruitful and multiply. Fill the earth and govern it.
Reign over the fish in the sea, the birds in the sky,
and all the animals that scurry along the ground.

GENESIS 1:27–28

A fascinating thing about your transformational journey is that what is happening internally is helping you to become everything God created you to be. The part of today's Scripture that speaks of God creating human beings in His own image always baffles me. I'm reminded of when my children were born and people would try to figure out who they looked like, only to decide they had characteristics of both of me and my husband. As they are getting older, I can look at them and see myself in them. I see myself in their eyes or how their face is forming. It is absolutely fascinating to watch them become individuals who reflect their father and me.

Just imagine God looking down on His children as they are moving about on the earth. I wonder if He longs to share with us how powerful we are through Him. I wonder if He sees some of us coming into who He created us to be and smiles like a loving Father. For others

of us who have lost our way, I know He is in pursuit of our hearts. He longs to show us His perspective, giving us an understanding of a divine nature that He can place inside us through the Holy Spirit. He longs to share in the journey of faith.

As you are being transformed, get quiet before God. He is releasing you not only into a new season but also into a greater version of who He has created you to be. Allow Him to make the grand reveal of the new you as He intended—free from past mistakes, sins, and condemnation. With your new mind, your new way of thinking, a clear heart and soul, you can walk in the divine authority that you always had, now with confidence and power.

Prayer

Father, I need You. I release the old version of me,
and I embrace the image of You in me. I embrace the way
You have always known me to be. Thank You.
In Jesus' name. Amen.

A Divine Plan

This was His eternal plan, which He carried out through Christ Jesus our Lord. Because of Christ and our faith in Him, we can now come boldly and confidently into God's presence.

EPHESIANS 3:11–12

When you picked up this devotional book, it was divinely planned. Throughout the last eighty-two days or so, the goal has always been to seek the Father. God has a divine plan that He's been carrying out from the beginning of time. God is executing His plans perfectly through the blood of Jesus. It has always been about redemption since the fall of man.

God longs to be reunited with us to share with us His plan and His purpose. Many people ask, "What is my purpose?" I've realized they are asking the wrong question. The question isn't "What is my purpose?" It's "What is God's purpose?" If you ever experience frustration in life from trying to find your purpose, realign yourself with God's plan. His purpose is clear. The next step is to ask God how you can best fulfill His purpose on earth within your area of influence. Once we come into this understanding, boldness and confidence naturally come with it. We realize more and more that who we are and what we were created to do is found in His purpose for us on the earth.

This takes daily surrendering. In today's world, we are bombarded by messages at every turn, whether it's social media, movies, billboards, or online ads. These messages can be loud and extremely influential. Have you ever thought about how these messages are impacting your life? It's so easy to let our thoughts drift these days! Why not ask God to reveal the ways your thought patterns are being altered by the messages that are flooding your pathways? Keep your prayer altar hot, stay in His Word, abide in His presence, and get ready to experience a life according to His purpose that you never even dreamed of.

Prayer

Father, give me boldness to walk confidently in who You have created me to be. Align me with Your purpose and not my own. In Jesus' name. Amen.

The Privilege of Prayer

For though we live in the world, we do not wage war
as the world does. The weapons we fight with are not
the weapons of the world. On the contrary, they have
divine power to demolish strongholds. We demolish arguments
and every pretension that sets itself up against the knowledge
of God, and we take captive every thought to make it
obedient to Christ.

II CORINTHIANS 10:3–5 NIV

It's easy to stay on the sidelines of faith, going to church and hearing about other believers doing amazing things for God. It is my hope that you, through reading this devotional book, have come to a place of transformation that has positioned you to soar in Christ. I would like to promise that it will be easy from here, but the truth is, God never promised us an easy life. However, we are always invited to sit at the feet of the Father and go to our place in prayer. That is our greatest weapon. Once you have identified what you need to release, you can go to the Creator of the universe and ask Him for the power, strength, and will to do so. Isn't that amazing? The God of it all longs to hear from us, to help us, and to give us everything we need to successfully complete His will for our lives.

God is giving out directions. Let's listen to Him! He can do more with our lives than we could ever think of or imagine—He can use our lives to make powerful impacts. Press your way into prayer, build your life around prayer, and make prayer more important than anything else. Through privilege of prayer, we get to know God and allow Him into our lives so that we know Him more. We get to build a real relationship with Him, through sharing our thoughts, struggles, and joys. We get to read His Word and understand His character. We get to reside in His presence. Through prayer, we can focus our eyes on God and what He wants for our lives. We can forget the things of the past and embrace the promises and purposes of the future.

Prayer

Father, I release every distraction that causes me to not pray. From this day forward I will center my life around hearing from You every single day. You are my priority. In Jesus' name. Amen.

An Unexpected Gift

Those who accept My commandments and obey them
are the ones who love Me. And because they love Me,
My Father will love them. And I will love them and reveal
Myself to each of them.

JOHN 14:21

When my husband and I first met, it was like we had known each other for years. The conversation flowed and we both knew early on that we were meant to be together. How? God revealed to us individually that we were meant to be together, and over time it was confirmed that we weren't caught up in infatuation with each other. We knew God had a divine will and plan for our life together.

During our engagement season, God revealed that my husband was a gift to me. I had a vision that God prepared a man who wasn't perfect but who was my person. A man who would love me through all my flaws and who would help me become the person God designed me to do be. Meeting my husband initially, however, came as a surprise to me. It was during a time when I was focused on growing closer to Christ. I no longer wanted to have an up-and-down relationship with Jesus. I no longer wanted to do my own thing, my own way. I was focused on being in complete alignment with Him and was not interested in dating anyone.

But as God would have it, I met my husband when I was trying to help a friend get connected to a young lady he was interested in. While I was focused on God, wanting to learn His commands and obey them, He brought me my husband. This is not the only time when I have seen the faithfulness of God in my life. Through the years, it has been in the consistency of obedience that I have experienced the heights of God that I never knew existed. I've been able to experience His love on the great level I've heard pastors and preachers talk about. But it has come with a price. The price of giving up my will for His. The price of obedience even when I had other desires or thoughts. The reward has been experiencing His love through kingdom principles. What about you? Can you think of time that God gave you a gift when you weren't expecting it? Take a moment to thank Him for that gift today. And if you can't think of a time, continue to align with Him, obey Him, and allow Him to reveal His love to you at the right time and place.

Prayer

Father, I want to know You more. I want to get into complete alignment with what You are doing in this season of my life. I release all fear holding me back. In Jesus' name. Amen.

Choose God

He is the one all the prophets testified about,
saying that everyone who believes in Him
will have their sins forgiven through His name.

ACTS 10:43

God's gift of forgiveness is just the beginning. The journey with God is a beautiful adventure. He introduces us to a life that works best when lived the way it was designed. Do you feel the need to be transformed? Are there habits, situations, relationships in your life that need to change? If so, how about taking these things to God in prayer? Ask Him to anything that goes against His ways. Dramatic transformation might not happen overnight. In fact, it might take years or even decades.

And when hard times hit, cling to God. True transformation in our lives doesn't happen on the mountaintop; it happens in hard times. It happens when we are pressed on all sides and we must make a decision. Choose Jesus every single time. Choose to seek Him in all you do. Choose to obey Him no matter how hard it gets. He is faithful and will never allow you to fall.

In hard times, God shows up in ways that only He can, and everyone around us will see the hand of God. Some people may never pick up a Bible before they come to know Jesus. They may only have your life as a testimony. What are they reading about Jesus through your life? What have they come to understand and know about Him? It's not that you have to be perfect, but the best course of action is always to choose Him. Let them ask why you always choose Jesus. Let them stand in awe and wonder of what God does in your life. That is how we transform the world.

Prayer

Father, make me light in the darkness. Show me who it is that I am influencing and give me the boldness to do as You lead and guide. In Jesus' name. Amen.

God's Timing

> *Blessed is the man who remains steadfast under trial,*
> *for when he has stood the test he will receive the crown of life,*
> *which God has promised to those who love him.*
>
> JAMES 1:12 ESV

Patience is something I've had to grow in. As a young adult, God would give me a vision or promise of what is to come, and instead of waiting for His direction or signal to move, I would run ahead of Him with passion and vigor. Almost every single time I would find myself confused and broken as to why things didn't work out the way I had planned. It was through prayer and maturity that I understood that God wanted me to wait. I had to believe the promise would come to pass, but in His timing. There was some testing and character-building I had to endure.

As a mother, I would never give my young kids the keys to drive my car. They would hurt themselves and others in the process of trying to drive. As a good Father, why would God allow us to have something before our time? What are you praying about currently that hasn't come to pass? Say it out loud. Why do you believe you haven't received it? If you don't know the answer to that question, ask God to reveal it to you.

Most of the time, when God does something for us, He is also thinking about how it can bless others around us. While there are gifts and promises that are for us, most of the time, the biggest blessings come in the form of a seed—a seed to sow into the lives of others. Does your promise only bless you? It is in these last few days of this book that I want you to get to the root of your motives. Ask God to reveal every area that you need purification in. It is there that I am praying that you receive transformation, clarity, and cleansing.

Prayer

Father, thank You for helping me see what I don't see. Open my eyes. I release the promises that I am standing on back to You. I want to make sure they are from Your thoughts, not my own. In Jesus' name. Amen.

Slowing Down

Jesus told her, "I am the resurrection and the life.
Anyone who believes in Me will live, even after dying.
Everyone who lives in Me and believes in Me
will never ever die. Do you believe this, Martha?"

JOHN 11:25–26

Today's Scripture passage introduces us to Martha. She was getting everything ready to go while her sister, Mary, sat with Jesus. I love this story of Mary and Martha because in our day and time, we can find ourselves inundated with things to do. We see the never-ending pile of laundry, the full-time job of meal planning for a family, and the marriage that needs attention, and we forget to start our day at the feet of Jesus.

God knows the things you need to get done, and He knows what you face each day. When we make it our mission to reside in the presence of God, we reprogram our minds away from overwhelm and toward belief. This belief is rooted in our faith and trust in Him. As we grow in our faith, we get into the habit of laying down our negative thoughts and ways and instead allow God to raise us up with new thoughts and ways to be His hands and feet on the earth.

Whenever you get into a bind, ask yourself, "What do I believe? What do I truly believe?" Your belief system is at the core of living a transformed life. You must believe in God! If you are having doubts and struggling to believe, ask Him to help you in that. When I am struggling to believe God in a certain area, I solicit the prayers of those who have the faith to believe for me until I can believe, too, or I speak God's Word out loud until I believe it. You can write four to five Scripture verses on sticky notes and put them somewhere you frequent. Then, every single day while you are standing by faith and believing God for something, rehearse these verses about you and your situation. Say it until you believe it!

Prayer

Father, our lives can feel so full at times. Help me slow down and be in Your presence. I release my schedule and my to-do list. I surrender my time to You, God. In Jesus' name. Amen.

Pray BIG

I tell you the truth, anyone who believes in Me
will do the same works I have done, and even greater works,
because I am going to be with the Father. You can ask for
anything in My name, and I will do it, so that the Son
can bring glory to the Father. Yes, ask Me for anything
in My name, and I will do it!

JOHN 14:12–14

This is a powerful moment. You have gone through eighty-eight days and four seasons of trusting God. Over the next few days, write down the things you want to ask God. These are the dreams and goals you now have after all the purifying, releasing, and cleansing He has done. We can be confident when we spend this much time with God that our hearts are positioned to pray for things that come into alignment with His perfect plans for us. God wants to get the glory out of your life. He longs for you to ask Him for anything, so think big. Think about the impossible thing you have doubted about yourself. While you are writing those things, make sure you pray today's Scripture passage. God loves to hear His Word spoken back to Him. He longs to know you are praying for things He has already spoken.

It is time that you step into the next level of your faith. If you can't think of any dreams or goals, ask God to remove the limitation on your mind. Sometimes we are unable to pray big because we can't conceive what that looks like. We can only pray within the confines of our environment or what we know. Ask God to expand your thinking of how much He can do in the life of a submitted vessel. Ask God to bring divine relationships that will help you grow and learn about areas of faith you have never experienced. Ask God for focus as you go forward through the process of asking for more. It is not a sin to ask for more. It is not a sin to believe in God for greater things. It is not a problem to believe a greater impact and influence is needed on the earth. Get to the root of the struggle of asking for more—and then release it.

Prayer

Father, I release the barrier preventing me from asking You for big things. If I am holding myself back from something You want to do in my life, show me that area.
In Jesus' name. Amen.

Stepping Out

My eager expectation and hope is that I will not be ashamed about anything, but that now as always, with all courage, Christ will be highly honored in my body, whether by life or by death.

PHILIPPIANS 1:20 CSB

Competing in a triathlon for the first time made me realize the barriers within my own mind. I understood that the reason I was not experiencing certain things in life was not because they weren't available to me but because I never allowed myself to reach for them. My boldness grew as I went into the unknown and into uncertainty, and I saw beauty in the midst of it. I now embrace the unknown with excitement because I have seen time and again how God uses these seasons to build boldness and endurance in me.

As someone who has always had a plan and believes in planning, I am no longer ashamed if my plans don't work out. What ends up happening is God's plan turns out much better for His glory. When I think back to all the things I wanted to do that didn't come about, I believe I would be living in frustration if I had held on to them, because while I would now have what I worked so hard for, I still would be unfulfilled on a deeper level. What about you? Do you feel relieved that God didn't allow some of your plans to work out?

Stepping out in faith and into the unknown is not easy. It leaves our loved ones wondering if something is wrong with us. They have good intentions and want to protect us, but we must seek God for understanding, confirmation, and clarity, not them. The best thing both sides can do is pray. Pray that we don't get distracted or miss God. But also pray that if we do miss God in this move, He will give us the grace to come back home and get it right.

Prayer

Father, my goal is to please You. May everyone I'm connected with have peace with what You are doing in my life. Thank You for my support system. In Jesus' name. Amen.

Sweet Release

Don't copy the behavior and customs of this world,
but let God transform you into a new person by changing the
way you think. Then you will learn to know God's will for you,
which is good and pleasing and perfect.

ROMANS 12:2

You made it to the last day. It is my prayer that your understanding about this next level of your relationship with God has changed. I pray that you now see God's kingdom in a new light. I pray that nothing and no one allows you to think you have sought anything other than Jesus. This transformation that we have been speaking of could only happen from within. It is in your personal walk with God that you have been experiencing a new level in Him every single day. The strongholds are no longer able to function in your life. It is now your mission to help others learn about who God is and help them come into the knowledge of His kingdom.

We must understand that our transformation is not for us and our lives only. Our transformation includes sharing God's love with others. If you know of someone who is wanting to step out in faith or needs encouragement to walk by faith, give them a copy of this book. Let them know how it helped you and what you experienced. Walk with them through it. Go deeper in the Scriptures. It is your turn, and it is your time. Your season is here. Do not let anyone tell you otherwise. If you have allowed God to cleanse your heart, maybe it's time to be a blessing to others. Give to the poor, forgive, keep your heart pure, and put God first. These are a few simple things to do to see this next level of your walk with God in a greater capacity than you could ever imagine. I'm excited for you. You are released!

Prayer

Father, thank You for the release. Help me free others from mental prisons. Help me represent You in every way so that I may help them experience true freedom in Christ. In Jesus' name. Amen.

DaySpring

LIVE YOUR FAITH

Dear Friend,

This book was prayerfully crafted with you, the reader, in mind. Every word, every sentence, every page was thoughtfully written, designed, and packaged to encourage you—right where you are this very moment. At DaySpring, our vision is to see every person experience the life-changing message of God's love. So, as we worked through rough drafts, design changes, edits, and details, we prayed for you to deeply experience His unfailing love, indescribable peace, and pure joy. It is our sincere hope that through these Truth-filled pages your heart will be blessed, knowing that God cares about you—your desires and disappointments, your challenges and dreams.

He knows. He cares. He loves you unconditionally.

BLESSINGS!
THE DAYSPRING BOOK TEAM

———————

Additional copies of this book and
other DaySpring titles can be purchased
at fine retailers everywhere.
Order online at <u>dayspring.com</u>
or
by phone at 1-877-751-4347